101 Crochet Stitch Patterns & Edgings

Patterns to create everything from doilies to afghans

Table of Contents

Before You Begin **2**

Swatches 1–77 .... **4–82**

A to Z Sampler Afghan **83**

Swatches 78–81 .... **86–90**

Patchwork Squares Afghan ... **91**

Edgings 82–101 .... **94–103**

Basics **104–125**

  Lesson 1: Getting Started 104

  Lesson 2: Chain Stitch 105

  Lesson 3: Working Into the Chain ... 107

  Lesson 4: Single Crochet 108

  Lesson 5: Double Crochet 111

  Lesson 6: Half Double Crochet 113

  Lesson 7: Treble Crochet 114

  Lesson 8: Slip Stitch 116

  Lesson 9: Stitch Sampler 117

  Lesson 10: Bead Crochet 117

  Lesson 11: Working With Colors 118

  Lesson 12: Working With Thread ... 119

  Lesson 13: Special Helps 120

  Lesson 14: Reading Patterns 124

  Lesson 15: Gauge 125

Crochet Stitch Guide **127**

Before You Begin

Unlike most crochet patterns, those in this book specify no gauge, no material requirements and no hook sizes.

That is because each stitch can be worked in your choice of yarn to vary the size and appearance of each stitch to fit your project.

The photos on pages 2 and 3 show Swatch 42 (page 47) worked in 3 different weights of yarn and 3 different hook sizes. You can see how the yarn will change the look of the stitch.

When choosing the material and hook for your project, you may wish to do some experimenting with a variety of materials until you achieve the appearance and texture that pleases you.

The stitch patterns photographed throughout this book were all made with worsted-weight yarn and a size I aluminum hook.

Working directly into afghan edge, single crochet edging is worked directly into the crochet fabric. Work one or more rounds of single crochet edging right around you afghan.

Begin by holding the afghan with right side facing you. Make a row of single crochet stitches into the edge, spacing the stitches evenly all the way around the afghan. Work 3 stitches into each corner or chain 2 for corner, join round with slip stitch into first single crochet.

#2 FINE WITH E HOOK

#4 WORSTED WITH H HOOK

Multiples

A multiple is the number of chains required for each repeat of the stitch pattern; to this we may then add a specified number of chains to make the pattern end correctly.

If a pattern specifies a multiple of 6 plus 2, for example, you need to make a starting chain in multiples of 6 (12, 18, 24, etc): then add a final 2 chains. The number of chains given after plus in a multiple is added only once.

Helpful Hint: When working a long foundation chain, add a few extra chains to ensure that the first row of the pattern will not run out of chains; then at the end of the first row, rip out any extra chains.

#5 BULKY WITH J HOOK

SWATCHES 1–47

Swatch 1

PATTERN NOTES

Made with 1 color of yarn.

Chain-2 at beginning of row or round counts as first half double crochet unless otherwise stated.

INSTRUCTIONS

Foundation ch: Ch multiple of 10 plus 6.

Row 1 (RS): Sl st in 2nd ch from hook and in each of next 4 chs, [hdc in each of next 5 chs, sl st in each of next 5 chs] across, turn.

Row 2: Remainder of piece is worked in **back lps** *(see Stitch Guide)*, sl st in each of first 5 sl sts, [hdc in each of next 5 hdc, sl st in each of next 5 sl sts] across, turn.

Row 3: Ch 2 *(see Pattern Notes)*, hdc in each of next 4 sl sts, [sl st in each of next 5 hdc, hdc in each of next 5 sl sts] across, turn.

Row 4: Ch 2, hdc in each of next 4 hdc, [sl st in each of next 5 sl sts, hdc in each of next 5 hdc] across, turn.

Row 5: Sl st in each of first 5 hdc, [hdc in each of next 5 sl sts, sl st in each of next 5 hdc] across, turn.

Rep rows 2–5 for pattern to desired length. At end of last row, **do not turn**. Fasten off. ▪

Swatch 2

PATTERN NOTE
Made with 3 colors.

SPECIAL STITCHES
Long double crochet (lng dc):
Yo, insert hook in next sc 2 rows below, yo, pull up lp even with working row, [yo, pull through 2 lps on hook] twice.

Extended long double crochet (ext lng dc): Yo, insert hook in next sc 3 rows below, yo, pull up lp even with working row, [yo, pull through 2 lps on hook] twice.

INSTRUCTIONS
Foundation ch: With first color, ch multiple of 33 plus 32.

Row 1 (RS): Sc in 2nd ch from hook and in each of next 14 chs, 3 sc in next ch, sc in each of next 15 chs, [sk next 2 chs, sc in each of next 15 chs, 3 sc in next ch, sc in each of next 15 chs] across, turn.

Row 2: Ch 1, sk first sc, sc in each of next 15 sc, 3 sc in next sc, [sc in each of next 15 sc, sk next 2 sc, sc in each of next 15 sc, 3 sc in next sc] across to last 16 sc, sc in each of next 14 sc, sk next sc, sc in last sc, turn.

Rows 3 & 4: Rep row 2. At end of row 4, **change color** (*see Stitch Guide*) to 2nd color by pulling lp through. Fasten off first color.

Row 5: Ch 1, sk first sc, *sc in next sc, **lng dc** (*see Special Stitches*), [sc in next sc, **ext lng dc** (*see Special Stitches*), sc in next sc, lng dc] 3 times, sc in next sc, 3 sc in next sc, sc in next sc, lng dc, [sc in next sc, ext lng dc, sc in next sc, lng dc] 3 times**, sc in next sc, sk next 2 sc, rep from * across, ending last rep at **, sk next sc, sc in last sc, turn.

Row 6: Ch 1, sk first sc, sc in each of next 15 sts, 3 sc in next sc, [sc in each of next 15 sts, sk next 2 sts, sc in each of next 15 sts, 3 sc in next sc] across to last 16 sts, sc in each of next 14 sts, sk next sc, sc in last sc, changing colors to first color in last st, turn. Fasten off 2nd color.

Rows 7–10: Rep row 2. At end of last row, change to 3rd color. Fasten off first color.

Rows 11 & 12: Rep rows 5 and 6. At end of last row, change to first color. Fasten off 3rd color.

Row 13: Rep row 2.

Rep rows 2–13 for pattern to desired length, ending last rep with row 10. At end of last row, fasten off. ▪

Swatch 3

PATTERN NOTES

Made with 1 color.

Chain-3 at beginning of row or round counts as first double crochet unless otherwise stated.

SPECIAL STITCHES

Cluster (cl): Holding back last lp of each dc on hook, 2 dc in next st, yo, pull through all lps on hook.

Front post cluster (fpcl): Holding back last lp of each dc on hook, 2 **fpdc** *(see Stitch Guide)* around next st, yo, pull through all lps on hook.

Back post cluster (bpcl): Holding back last lp of each dc on hook, 2 **bpdc** *(see Stitch Guide)* around next st, yo, pull through all lps on hook.

INSTRUCTIONS

Foundation ch: Ch multiple of 6 plus 3.

Row 1 (RS): (2 dc, ch 2, 2 dc) in 6th ch from hook *(first 5 chs count as first dc, sk 2 chs)*, [sk next 2 chs, **cl** *(see Special Stitches)* in next ch, sk next 2 chs, (2 dc, ch 2, 2 dc) in next ch] across to last 3 chs, sk next 2 chs, dc in last ch, turn.

Row 2: Ch 3 *(see Pattern Notes)*, [(2 dc, ch 2, 2 dc) in next ch-2 sp, **bpcl** *(see Special Stitches)* around next cl] across to last ch-2 sp, (2 dc, ch

2, 2 dc) in last ch-2 sp, sk next 2 dc, dc in 5th ch of beg 5 chs, turn.

Row 3: Ch 3, [(2 dc, ch 2, 2 dc) in next ch-2 sp, **fpcl** *(see Special Stitches)* around next bpcl] across to last ch-2 sp, (2 dc, ch 2, 2 dc) in last ch-2 sp, sk next 2 dc, dc in last st, turn.

Row 4: Ch 3, [(2 dc, ch 2, 2 dc) in next ch-2 sp, bpcl around next fpcl] across to last ch-2 sp, (2 dc, ch 2, 2 dc) in last ch-2 sp, sk next 2 dc, dc in last st, turn.

Rep rows 3 and 4 for pattern to desired length. Fasten off. ▪

Swatch 4

PATTERN NOTE
Made with 1 color.

INSTRUCTIONS
Foundation ch: Ch multiple of 8 plus 2.

Row 1 (RS): Sc in 2nd ch from hook and in each ch across, turn.

Row 2: Ch 1, (sc, 3 dc) in first sc, [sk next 3 sc, (sc, 3 dc) in next sc] across to last 4 sc, sk next 3 sc, sc in last sc, turn.

Row 3: Ch 1, (sc, 3 dc) in first sc, [sk next 3 dc, (sc, 3 dc) in next sc] across to last sc, sc in last sc, turn.

Rep row 3 for pattern to desired length. Fasten off. ▪

Swatch 5

PATTERN NOTES

Made with 1 color.

Chain-3 at beginning of row or round counts as first double crochet unless otherwise stated.

Chain-5 at beginning of row or round counts as first double crochet and chain-2 unless otherwise stated.

Chain-4 at beginning of row or round counts as first double crochet and chain-1 unless otherwise stated.

INSTRUCTIONS

Foundation ch: Ch multiple of 6 plus 3.

Row 1 (RS): Sc in 2nd ch from hook and in next ch, [ch 4, sk next 4 chs, sc in each of next 2 chs] across, turn.

Row 2: Ch 3 (*see Pattern Notes*), (2 dc, ch 2, 2 dc) in next ch-4 sp and in each ch-4 sp across to last 2 sc, sk next sc, dc in last sc, turn.

Row 3: Ch 5 (*see Pattern Notes*), 2 sc in next ch-2 sp, [ch 4, 2 sc in next ch-2 sp] across, ch 2, dc in last st, turn.

Row 4: Ch 4 (*see Pattern Notes*), 2 dc in next ch-2

sp, (2 dc, ch 2, 2 dc) in each ch-4 sp across to last ch sp, 2 dc in last ch sp, ch 1, dc in last st, turn.

Row 5: Ch 3, dc in next ch-1 sp, ch 4, [2 dc in next ch-2 sp, ch 4] across to last ch-1 sp, dc in next ch-1 sp, dc in last st, turn.

Row 6: Ch 3, (2 dc, ch 2, 2 dc) in each ch-4 sp across to last 2 dc, sk next dc, dc in last st, turn.

Rep rows 3–6 consecutively for pattern to desired length. Fasten off. ▪

Swatch 6

PATTERN NOTES

Made with 1 color.

Chain-3 at beginning of row or round counts as first double crochet unless otherwise stated.

Chain-2 at beginning of row or round counts as first half double crochet unless otherwise stated.

SPECIAL STITCH

Cluster (cl): Holding back last lp of each st on hook, 2 dc as indicated in instructions, yo, pull through all lps on hook.

INSTRUCTIONS

Foundation ch: Ch multiple of 3 plus 6.

Row 1 (RS): Dc in 4th ch from hook (*first 3 chs count as first dc*) and in each ch across, turn.

Row 2: Ch 2 (*see Pattern Notes*), hdc in each st across, turn.

Row 3: Ch 3 (*see Pattern Notes*), dc in same hdc as beg ch-3, ch 3, **cl** (*see Special Stitch*) in top of dc just made, sk next hdc, [**dc dec** (*see Stitch Guide*) in next 3 hdc, ch 3, cl in top of dc dec just made] across to last 2 hdc, dc dec in last 2 hdc, turn.

Row 4: Ch 3, dc in same st as beg ch-3, [3 dc in top of next dc dec] across to last st, 2 dc in last st, turn.

Row 5: Ch 3, dc in each dc across, turn.

Row 6: Ch 2, hdc in each dc across, turn.

Rep rows 3–6 consecutively for pattern to desired length. Fasten off. ▪

Swatch 7

PATTERN NOTES
Made with 3 colors.

Color sequence: 2 rows of each color
ending with 2 rows of first color.

INSTRUCTIONS
Foundation ch: With first color,
ch multiple of 24 plus 26.

Foundation ch of at least 50 is
necessary to work sample swatch.

Row 1 (RS): Dc in 5th ch from hook
and in each of next 3 chs, [2 dc in
next ch, dc in next ch] 6 times, *dc
in each of next 3 chs, sk next 2 chs,
dc in next ch, sk next 2 chs, dc in
each of next 4 chs, [2 dc in next ch,
dc in next ch] 6 times, rep from * across to last
6 chs, dc in each of next 3 chs, sk next 2 chs, dc
in last ch, turn.

Row 2: Ch 2, sk next 3 dc, working in **back lps**
(*see Stitch Guide*), dc in each of next 4 dc, [2
dc in next dc, dc in next dc] 6 times, *dc in
each of next 3 dc, sk next 3 dc, **fpdc** (*see Stitch
Guide*) around next dc, sk next 3 dc, dc in each
of next 4 dc, [2 dc in next dc, dc in next dc] 6
times, rep from * across to last 6 dc, dc in each
of next 3 dc, sk last 3 dc, dc in next ch of beg 4
chs, **change color** (*see Stitch Guide and Pattern
Notes*) to next color by pulling lp through, turn.
Fasten off first color.

Row 3: Ch 2, sk next 3 dc, working in back lps,
dc in each of next 4 dc, [2 dc in next dc, dc in
next dc] 6 times, *dc in each of next 3 dc, sk
next 3 dc, **bpdc** (*see Stitch Guide*) around next
fpdc, sk next st on this row behind bpdc,
sk next 3 dc, dc in each of next 4 dc, [2 dc in
next dc, dc in next dc] 6 times, rep from *
across to last 6 dc, dc in each of next 3 dc, sk
last 3 dc, dc in 2nd ch of turning ch-2, turn.

Row 4: Ch 2, sk next 3 dc, working in back lps,
dc in each of next 4 dc, [2 dc in next dc, dc in
next dc] 6 times, *dc in each of next 3 dc, sk
next 3 dc, fpdc around next bpdc, sk next st
on this row behind fpdc, sk next 3 dc, dc in
each of next 4 dc, [2 dc in next dc, dc in next
dc] 6 times, rep from * across to last 6 dc, dc in
each of next 3 dc, sk last 3 dc, dc in 2nd ch of
turning ch-2, change to next color by pulling lp
through, turn. Fasten off 2nd color

Working in **color sequence** (*see Pattern Notes*),
rep rows 3 and 4 alternately for desired length.
Fasten off. ∎

Swatch 8

PATTERN NOTES
Made with 1 color.

Chain-2 at beginning of row or round counts as first double crochet unless otherwise stated.

INSTRUCTIONS
Foundation ch: Ch multiple of 8 plus 3.

Row 1 (RS): Dc in 3rd ch from hook (*first 2 chs count as first dc*) and in each ch across, turn.

Row 2: Ch 2 (*see Pattern Notes*), [**fpdc** (*see Stitch Guide*) around each of next 4 dc, **bpdc** (*see Stitch Guide*) around each of next 4 dc] across, ending with dc in last st, turn.

Row 3: Ch 2, bpdc around next st, fpdc around each of next 4 sts, [bpdc around each of next 4 sts, fpdc around each of next 4 sts] across to last 4 sts, bpdc around each of next 3 sts, dc in last st, turn.

Row 4: Ch 2, fpdc around each of next 2 sts, bpdc around each of next 4 sts, [fpdc around each of next 4 sts, bpdc around each of next 4 sts] to last 3 sts, fpdc around each of next 2 sts, dc in last st, turn.

Row 5: Ch 2, bpdc around each of next 3 sts, fpdc around each of next 4 sts, [bpdc around each of next 4 sts, fpdc around each of next 4 sts] across to last 2 sts, bpdc around next st, dc in last st, turn.

Row 6: Ch 2, [bpdc around each of next 4 sts, fpdc around each of next 4 sts] across to last st, dc in last st, turn.

Row 7: Ch 2, fpdc around next st, bpdc around each of next 4 sts, [fpdc around each of next 4 sts, bpdc around each of next 4 sts] across to last 4 sts, fpdc around each of next 3 sts, dc in last st, turn.

Row 8: Ch 2, bpdc around each of next 2 sts, fpdc around each of next 4 sts, [bpdc around each of next 4 sts, fpdc around each of next 4 sts] across to last 3 sts, bpdc around each of next 2 sts, dc in last st, turn.

Row 9: Ch 2, fpdc around each of next 3 sts, bpdc around each of next 4 sts, [fpdc around each of next 4 sts, bpdc around each of next 4 sts] across to last 2 sts, fpdc around next st, dc in last st, turn.

Row 10: Ch 2, [fpdc around each of next 4 sts, bpdc around each of next 4 sts] across to last st, dc in last st, turn.

Rep rows 3–10 consecutively for desired length. Fasten off. ▪

Swatch 9

PATTERN NOTES
Made with 1 color.

Chain-2 at beginning of row or round counts as first double crochet unless otherwise stated.

SPECIAL STITCH
Bobble: Holding back last lp of each st on hook, 5 tr as indicated in instructions, yo, pull through all lps on hook.

INSTRUCTIONS
Foundation ch: Ch multiple of 12 plus 6.

Row 1 (RS): Sc in 2nd ch from hook and in next ch, [ch 1, sk next ch, sc in each of next 11 chs] across to last 3 chs, ch 1, sk next ch, sc in each of last 2 chs, turn.

Row 2: Ch 2 *(see Pattern Notes)*, dc in next sc, [ch 1, sk next ch-1 sp, dc in each of next 11 sts] across to last ch-1 sp, ch 1, sk last ch-1 sp, dc in each of last 2 sc, turn.

Row 3: Ch 1, sc in each of first 2 dc, **bobble** *(see Special Stitch)* in next ch-1 sp 2 rows below, sc in next dc on this row, [ch 1, sk next dc, sc in each of next 7 dc, ch 1, sk next dc, sc in next dc, bobble in next ch-1 sp 2 rows below, sc in next dc on this row] across to last st, sc in last st, turn.

Row 4: Ch 2, dc in each of next 3 sts, [ch 1, sk next ch-1 sp, dc in each of next 7 sts, ch 1, sk next ch-1 sp, dc in each of next 3 sts] to last sc, dc in last sc, turn.

Row 5: Ch 1, sc in each of first 4 dc, [bobble in next ch-1 sp 2 rows below, sc in next dc on this row, ch 1, sk next dc, sc in each of next 3 dc, ch 1, sk next dc, sc in next dc, bobble in next ch-1 sp 2 rows below, sc in each of next 3 dc on this row] across to last st, sc in last st, turn.

Row 6: Ch 2, dc in each of next 5 sts, [ch 1, sk next ch-1 sp, dc in each of next 3 sts, ch 1, sk next ch-1 sp, dc in each of next 7 sts] across to last 2 ch-1 sps, ch 1, sk next ch-1 sp, dc in each of next 3 sts, ch 1, sk next ch-1 sp, dc in each of last 6 sts, turn.

Row 7: Ch 1, sc in each of first 6 dc, [bobble in next ch-1 sp 2 rows below, sc in next dc on this row, ch 1, sk next dc, sc in next dc, bobble in next ch-1 sp 2 rows below, sc in each of next 7 dc on this row] across to last 2 ch-1 sps 2 rows below, bobble in next ch-1 sp 2 rows below, sc in next dc on this row, ch 1, sk next dc, sc in next dc, bobble in next ch-1 sp 2 rows below, sc in each of last 6 sts on this row, turn.

Row 8: Ch 2, dc in each of next 7 sts, ch 1, sk next ch-1 sp, [dc in each of next 11 sts, ch 1, sk next ch-1 sp] across to last 8 sts, dc in each of last 8 sts, turn.

Row 9: Ch 1, sc in each of first 6 dc, ch 1, sk next dc, sc in next dc, [bobble in next ch-1 sp 2 rows below, sc in next dc on this row, ch 1, sk next dc, sc in each of next 7 dc, ch 1, sk next dc, sc in next dc] across to last ch-1 sp 2 rows below, bobble in last ch-1 sp 2 rows below, sc in next dc on this row, ch 1, sk next dc, sc in each of last 6 dc, turn.

Row 10: Rep row 6.

Row 11: Ch 1, sc in each of first 4 dc, [ch 1, sk next dc, sc in next dc, bobble in next ch-1 sp 2 rows below, sc in each of next 3 dc on this row, bobble in next ch-1 sp 2 rows below, sc in next dc on this row, ch 1, sk next dc, sc in each of next 3 dc] across to last st, sc in last st, turn.

Row 12: Rep row 4.

Row 13: Ch 1, sc in each of first 2 dc, ch 1, sk next dc, sc in next dc, [bobble in next ch-1 sp 2 rows below, sc in each of next 7 dc on this row, bobble in next ch-1 sp 2 rows below, sc in next dc on this row, ch 1, sk next dc, sc in next dc] across to last dc, sc in last dc, turn.

Row 14: Rep row 2.

Next rows: Rep rows 3–14 consecutively for desired length.

Last row: Ch 1, sc in each of first 2 dc, [bobble in next ch-1 sp 2 rows below, sc in each of next 11 dc on this row] across to last ch-1 sp 2 rows below, bobble in last ch-1 sp 2 rows below, sc in each of last 2 dc on this row. Fasten off. ▪

Swatch 10

PATTERN NOTES
Made with 1 color.

Chain-2 at beginning of row or round counts as first double crochet unless otherwise stated.

INSTRUCTIONS
Foundation ch: Ch multiple of 6 plus 3.

Row 1 (RS): Dc in 3rd ch from hook (*first 2 chs count as first dc*) and in each ch across, turn.

Row 2: Ch 2 (*see Pattern Notes*), [**fpdc** (*see Stitch Guide*) around each of next 3 dc, **bpdc** (*see Stitch Guide*) around each of next 3 dc] across to last st, dc in last st, turn.

Row 3: Ch 2, [fpdc around each of next 3 bpdc, bpdc around each of next 3 fpdc] across to last st, dc in last st, turn.

Row 4: Ch 2, [bpdc around each of next 3 bpdc, fpdc around each of next 3 fpdc] across to last st, dc in last st, turn.

Row 5: Ch 2, [bpdc around each of next 3 fpdc, fpdc around each of next 3 bpdc] across to last st, dc in last st, turn.

Row 6: Ch 2, [fpdc around each of next 3 fpdc, bpdc around each of next 3 bpdc] across to last st, dc in last st, turn.

Rep rows 3–6 consecutively for pattern to desired length, ending with row 3. At end of last row, fasten off. ▪

Swatch 11

PATTERN NOTES
Made with 1 color.

Chain-2 at beginning of row or
round counts as first double crochet
unless otherwise stated.

SPECIAL STITCH
Circle: 6 fpdc around next dc, turn
piece upside down, 6 fpdc around
previous dc on same row.

INSTRUCTIONS
Foundation ch: Ch multiple of
10 plus 1.

Row 1 (RS): Dc in 3rd ch from hook
(*first 2 chs count as first dc*) and in
each ch across, turn.

Row 2: Ch 2 (*see Pattern Notes*),
dc in each dc across, turn.

Row 3: Ch 2, dc in each of next 4 dc, work **circle**
(*see Special Stitch*), [working behind circle, dc
in top of same dc as beg part of circle made and
in each of next 9 dc, work circle] across to last
5 sts, dc in top of same dc as beg part of circle
made and in each of last 4 sts, turn.

Row 4: Ch 2, dc in each st across, turn.

Rows 5 & 6: Rep row 4.

Row 7: Ch 2, dc in each of next 9 dc, work circle,
[working behind circle, dc in top of same dc
as beg part of circle made and in each of next
9 dc, work circle] across to last 10 sts, working
behind circle, dc in top of same dc as beg part
of circle made and in each of last 9 dc, turn.

Rows 8–10: Rep row 4.

Rep rows 3–10 consecutively for pattern to
desired length, ending with row 4. At end of
last row, fasten off. ▪

Swatch 12

PATTERN NOTES
Made with 1 color.

Chain-2 at beginning of row or round counts as first double crochet unless otherwise stated.

SPECIAL STITCH
Shell: (2 dc, ch 1, 2 dc) as indicated in instructions.

INSTRUCTIONS
Foundation ch: Ch multiple of 16 plus 18.

Row 1 (RS): Sc in 2nd ch from hook, [ch 5, sk next 3 chs, sc in next ch] across, turn.

Row 2: Ch 4, *(counts as first dc and ch-2)*, sc in next ch-5 sp, ch 5, sc in next ch-5 sp, **shell** *(see Special Stitch)* in next sc, *[sc in next ch-5 sp, ch 5] 3 times, sc in next ch-5 sp, shell in next sc, rep from * across to last 2 ch-5 sps, sc in next ch-5 sp, ch 5, sc in last ch-5 sp, ch 2, dc in last sc, turn.

Row 3: Ch 1, sc in first dc, ch 5, sc in next ch-5 sp, shell in next sc, sc in next ch-1 sp, shell in next sc, *[sc in next ch-5 sp, ch 5] twice, sc in next ch-5 sp, shell in next sc, sc in next ch-1 sp, shell in next sc, rep from * to last ch-5 sp, sc in last ch-5 sp, ch 5, sk next 2 chs of turning ch-4, sc in next ch of turning ch, turn.

Row 4: Ch 4, sc in next ch-5 sp, shell in next sc, sc in next ch-1 sp, ch 5, sc in next ch-1 sp, shell in next sc, sc in next ch-5 sp, [ch 5, sc in next ch-5 sp, shell in next sc, sc in next ch-1 sp, ch 5, sc in next ch-1 sp, shell in next sc, sc in next ch-5 sp] across to last sc, ch 2, dc in last sc, turn.

Row 5: Ch 1, sc in first dc, shell in next sc, sc in next ch-1 sp, ch 5, sc in next ch-5 sp, ch 5, sc in next ch-1 sp, shell in next sc, [sc in next ch-5 sp, shell in next sc, sc in next ch-1 sp, ch 5, sc in next ch-5 sp, ch 5, sc in next ch-1 sp, shell in next sc] across to turning ch, sc in sp formed by turning ch-4, turn.

Row 6: **Ch 2** *(see Pattern Notes)*, 2 dc in same sc as beg ch-2, sc in next ch-1 sp, ch 5, sc in next ch-5 sp, shell in next sc, sc in next ch-5 sp, ch 5, sc in next ch-1 sp, [shell in next sc, sc in next ch-1 sp, ch 5, sc in next ch-5 sp, shell in next sc, sc in next ch-5 sp, ch 5, sc in next ch-1 sp] across to last sc, 3 dc in last sc, turn.

Row 7: Ch 1, sc in first dc, ch 5, sc in next ch-5 sp, shell in next sc, sc in next ch-1 sp, shell in next sc, sc in next ch-5 sp, ch 5, [sc in next ch-1 sp, ch 5, sc in next ch-5 sp, shell in next sc, sc in next ch-1 sp, shell in next sc, sc in next ch-5 sp, ch 5] across to turning ch, sc in 2nd ch of turning ch-2, turn.

Rep rows 4–7 consecutively for pattern to desired length, ending with row 6. At end of last row, fasten off. ▪

Swatch 13

PATTERN NOTE
Made with 1 color.

SPECIAL STITCHES
Beginning cluster (beg cl): Yo, pull up lp in next sc, [yo, pull up lp in next dc] 3 times, [yo, pull up lp in next sc] 4 times, yo, pull through all lps on hook.

Cluster (cl): Working in unworked lps of next 4 chs, [yo, pull up lp in next ch] 4 times, [yo, pull up lp in next dc] 3 times, yo, pull up lp in next sc, [yo, pull up lp in next dc] 3 times, [yo, pull up lp in next sc] 4 times, yo, pull through all lps on hook.

Half cluster (half cl): Working in unworked lps of next 4 chs, [yo, pull up lp in next ch] 4 times, [yo, pull up lp in next dc] 3 times, yo, pull up lp in next sc, yo, pull through all lps on hook.

INSTRUCTIONS
Foundation ch: Ch multiple of 8 plus 13.

Row 1 (RS): Sc in 2nd ch from hook and in each of next 3 chs, sk next 3 chs, 3 dc in next ch, sk next 3 chs, sc in next ch, [sk next 3 chs, (3 dc, ch 5, sc in 2nd ch from hook and in each of next 3 chs, 3 dc) in next ch, sk next 3 chs, sc in next ch] across, turn.

Row 2 (RS): Ch 4, **beg cl** (*see Special Stitches*) in next 8 sts, [ch 4, sc in sk ch of next ch-5, ch 3, **cl** (*see Special Stitches*) in next 15 sts] across to beg sk ch, ch 4, sc in sk ch, turn.

Row 3: Ch 1, sc in next sc, [(3 dc, ch 5, sc in 2nd ch from hook and in next 3 chs, 3 dc) in next cl, sc in next sc] across to beg cl, 4 dc in beg cl, turn.

Row 4: Ch 8, beg in 5th ch from hook, [yo, pull up lp in next ch] 4 times, [yo, pull up lp in next dc] 4 times, yo, pull up lp in next sc, [yo, pull up lp in next dc] 3 times, [yo, pull up lp in next sc] 4 times, yo and pull through all lps on hook, ch 4, sc in sk ch of next ch-5, ch 3, [cl, ch 4, sc in sk ch of next ch-5, ch 3] across to last ch-5, sc in sk ch of last ch-5, **half cl** (*see Special Stitches*), turn.

Row 5: Ch 8, sc in 2nd ch from hook and in each of next 3 chs, 3 dc in next half cl, sc in next sc, [(3 dc, ch 5, sc in 2nd ch from hook and in next 3 chs, 3 dc) in next cl, sc in next sc] across to turning ch, sc in 5th ch of turning ch-8, turn.

Rep rows 2–5 consecutively for pattern to desired length.

At end of last row, fasten off. ▪

Swatch 14

PATTERN NOTES

Made with 2 colors.

Chain-2 at beginning of row or round counts as first double crochet unless otherwise stated.

INSTRUCTIONS

Foundation ch: With first color, ch multiple of 8 plus 11.

Row 1 (RS): 2 dc in 3rd ch from hook *(first 2 chs count as first dc)*, sk next 3 chs, sc in next ch, [sk next 3 chs, 5 dc in next ch, sk next 3 chs, sc in next ch] across to last 4 chs, sk next 3 chs, 3 dc in last ch, **changing color** *(see Stitch Guide)* to 2nd color in last st, turn. Fasten off first color.

Row 2: Ch 1, sc in first dc, ch 3, **dc dec** *(see Stitch Guide)* in next 5 sts, ch 3, [sc in next dc, ch 3, dc dec in next 5 chs, ch 3] across ending with sc in last st, turn.

Row 3: Ch 2 *(see Pattern Notes)* in same st as beg ch-2, sc in next dc dec, [5 dc in next sc, sc in next dc dec] across to last sc, 3 dc in last sc, changing to first color in last st, turn. Fasten off 2nd color.

Row 4: Ch 1, sc in first st, ch 3, dc dec in next 5 sts, [ch 3, sc in next dc, ch 3, dc dec in next 5 sts] across, ending with ch 3, sc in last st, turn.

Row 5: Ch 2, 2 dc in same st as beg ch-2, sc in next dc dec, [5 dc in next sc, sc in next dc dec] across, ending with 3 dc in last st, changing to 2nd color in last st, turn. Fasten off first color.

Working in established color sequence, rep rows 4 and 5 alternately for desired length. At end of last row, fasten off. ▪

Swatch 15

PATTERN NOTE
Made with 1 color.

SPECIAL STITCH
Puff stitch (puff st): Ch 4, 2 dc in 4th ch from hook.

INSTRUCTIONS
Foundation ch: Ch multiple of 4 plus 2.

Row 1 (RS): Sc in 2nd ch from hook, [ch 1, sk next ch, sc in next ch] across, turn.

Row 2: Ch 1, sc in first sc, [**puff st** *(see Special Stitch)*, sc in next sc, ch 1, sc in next sc] across, turn.

Row 3: Ch 1, sc in first sc, [ch 1, sc in next sc, ch 1, working behind puff st, sc in next sc] across, turn.

Row 4: Ch 1, sc in first sc, [ch 1, sc in next sc] across, turn.

Row 5: Rep row 4.

Row 6: Ch 1, sc in first sc, [ch 1, sc in next sc, puff st, sc in next sc] across, turn.

Row 7: Ch 1, sc in first sc, [ch 1, working behind puff st, sc in next sc, ch 1, sc in next sc] across, turn.

Rows 8 & 9: Rep row 4.

Rep rows 2–9 consecutively for pattern to desired length, ending with row 5. At end of last row, fasten off. ▪

Swatch 16

PATTERN NOTES
Made with 1 color.

Chain-6 at beginning of row or round counts as first treble crochet and chain 2 unless otherwise stated.

SPECIAL STITCH
Cluster (cl): Holding back last lp of each st on hook, 2 dc as indicated in instructions, yo, pull through all lps on hook.

INSTRUCTIONS
Foundation ch: Ch multiple of 20 plus 18.

Row 1 (RS): Sc in 2nd ch from hook, [ch 5, sk next 3 chs, sc in next ch] across, turn.

Row 2: Ch 6 (*see Pattern Notes*), sc in next ch-5 sp, ch 5, sc in next ch-5 sp, (**cl**—*see Special Stitch*, ch 3, cl) in next sc, *sc in next ch-5 sp, [ch 5, sc in next ch-5 sp] 4 times, (cl, ch 3, cl) in next sc, rep from * across to last ch-5 sp, sc in last ch-5 sp, ch 2, tr in last sc, turn.

Row 3: Ch 1, sc in next tr, ch 5, sc in next ch-5 sp, *(cl, ch 3, cl) in next sc, sc in next ch-3 sp, (cl, ch 3, cl) in next sc, sc in next ch-5 sp, [ch 5, sc in next ch-5 sp] 3 times, rep from * across to turning ch, ch 5, sc in 4th ch of turning ch-6, turn.

Row 4: Ch 6, sc in next ch-5 sp, ch 5, sc in next ch-3 sp, *(cl, ch 3, cl) in next sc, sc in next ch-3 sp, [ch 5, sc in next ch-5 sp] 3 times, ch 5, sc in next ch-3 sp, rep from * across to last ch-5 sp, ch 5, sc in last ch-5 sp, ch 2, tr in last sc, turn.

Row 5: Ch 1, sc in next tr, *ch 5, sc in next ch-5 sp, ch 5, sc in next ch-3 sp, [ch 5, sc in next ch-5 sp] twice, (cl, ch 3, cl) in next sc, sc in next ch-5 sp, rep from * across to turning ch, ch 5, sc in 4th ch of turning ch-6, turn.

Row 6: Ch 6, *sc in next ch-5 sp, [ch 5, sc in next ch-5 sp] 3 times, (cl, ch 3, cl) in next sc, sc in next ch-3 sp, (cl, ch 3, cl) in next sc, rep from * across to last sc, ch 2, tr in last sc, turn.

Row 7: Ch 1, sc in next tr, *[ch 5, sc in next ch-5 sp] 3 times, ch 5, sc in next ch-3 sp, (cl, ch 3, cl) in next sc, sc in next ch-3 sp, rep from * across to turning ch, ch 5, sc in 4th ch of turning ch-6, turn.

Row 8: Ch 6, sc in next ch-5 sp, ch 5, sc in next ch-5 sp, *(cl, ch 3, cl) in next sc, [sc in next ch-5 sp, ch 5] twice, sc in next ch-3 sp, [ch 5, sc in next ch-5 sp] twice, rep from * across to last sc, ch 2, tr in last sc, turn.

Rep rows 3–8 consecutively for pattern to desired length. At end of last row, fasten off. ▪

Swatch 17

PATTERN NOTES
Made with 1 color.

Chain-3 at beginning of row or round counts as first double crochet unless otherwise stated.

SPECIAL STITCH
Cluster (cl): Yo, pull up lp in next st, [yo, pull up lp in same st] twice, yo, pull through all lps on hook.

INSTRUCTIONS
Foundation ch: Ch multiple of 17 plus 3.

Row 1 (RS): Dc in 5th ch from hook, [**dc dec** (see Stitch Guide) in next 2 chs] twice, ch 1, [**cl** (see Special Stitch) in next ch, ch 1] 5 times, *[dc dec in next 2 chs] 6 times, ch 1, [cl in next ch, ch 1] 5 times, rep from * across to last 6 chs, [dc dec in next 2 chs] 3 times, turn.

Row 2: Ch 1, sc in each st and in each ch across to last dc, sc in last dc, turn.

Row 3: Ch 3 (see Pattern Notes), dc in next sc, [dc dec in next 2 sc] twice, *ch 1, [cl in next sc, ch 1] 5 times, [dc dec in next 2 sts] 6 times, rep from * across to last 6 sc, [dc dec in next 2 sc] 3 times, turn.

Rep rows 2 and 3 alternately for pattern to desired length. At end of last row, fasten off. ▪

Swatch 18

PATTERN NOTES

Made with 1 color.

Chain-3 at beginning of row or round counts as first treble crochet unless otherwise stated.

INSTRUCTIONS

Foundation ch: Ch multiple of 8 plus 2.

Row 1 (WS): Sc in 2nd ch from hook, [sk next 3 chs, 7 tr in next ch, sk next 3 chs, sc in next ch] across, turn.

Row 2 (RS): Ch 1, sc in first sc, [**bpsc** *(see Stitch Guide)* around each of next 7 tr, sc in next sc] across, turn.

Row 3: **Ch 3** *(see Pattern Notes)*, 3 tr in same st as beg ch-3, sk next 3 sts, sc in next st, sk next 3 sts, [7 tr in next sc, sk next 3 sts, sc in next st, sk next 3 sts] across to last sc, 4 tr in last sc, turn.

Row 4: Ch 1, sc in first tr, bpsc around each of next 3 tr, sc in next sc, [bpsc around each of next 7 tr, sc in next sc] across to last 4 sts, bpsc around each of next 3 tr, sc in 3rd ch of turning ch-3, turn.

Row 5: Ch 1, sc in first sc, [sk next 3 sts, 7 tr in next sc, sk next 3 sts, sc in next st] across, turn.

Row 6: Ch 1, sc in first sc, [bpsc around each of next 7 tr, sc in next sc] across, turn.

Rep rows 3–6 consecutively for pattern to desired length. At end of last row, fasten off. ∎

Swatch 19

PATTERN NOTE
Made with 2 colors.

SPECIAL STITCH
Decrease (dec): Holding back last lp of each st on hook, dtr in next dc, sk next sc, dtr in next st, yo, pull through all lps on hook.

INSTRUCTIONS
Foundation ch: With first color, ch multiple of 12 plus 14.

Row 1 (WS): Sc in 2nd ch from hook, and in next ch, [ch 1, sk next ch, sc in next ch] across, ending with sc in last ch, turn.

Row 2 (RS): Ch 1, sc in first sc, sc in next ch-1 sp, (tr, ch 1) 4 times in next ch-1 sp, *sk next ch-1 sp, [sc in next ch-1 sp, ch 1] 3 times, sk next ch-1 sp, (tr, ch 1) 4 times in next ch-1 sp, rep from * across to last 2 ch-1 sps, sk next ch-1 sp, sc in last ch-1 sp, ch 1, sk next sc, sc in last sc, turn.

Row 3: Ch 1, sc in first sc, [dc in next sc, ch 1, dc in next tr, ch 1, (dc, ch 1) twice in each of next 2 tr, dc in next tr, ch 1, dc in next sc, sc in next sc] across, **changing color** (see Stitch Guide) in last st to 2nd color, turn. Fasten off first color.

Row 4: Ch 4, dtr in next dc, tr in next dc, ch 1, dc in next dc, ch 1, [sc in next dc, ch 1] twice, dc in next dc, ch 1, tr in next dc, sk next ch-1 sp, **dec** (see Special Stitch) in next 3 sts, tr in next dc, ch 1, dc in next dc, ch 1, [sc in next dc, ch 1] twice, dc in next dc, ch 1, tr in next dc, *dec in next 3 sts, tr in next dc, ch 1, dc in next dc, ch 1, [sc in next dc, ch 1] twice, dc in next dc, ch 1, tr in next dc, rep from * to last 2 sts, **dtr dec** (see Stitch Guide) in last 2 sts, turn.

Row 5: Ch 1, sc in first st and in next tr, [ch 1, sk next ch-1 sp, sc in next st] 5 times, *ch 1, sk next st and next ch-1 sp, sc in next st, [ch 1, sk next ch-1 sp, sc in next st] 5 times, rep from * across to last dtr, sk last dtr, sc in next ch of turning ch-4, changing color to first color in last st, turn. Fasten off 2nd color.

Rep rows 2–5 consecutively for pattern to desired length. At end of last row, fasten off. ▪

Swatch 20

PATTERN NOTES

Made with 1 color.

Chain-4 at beginning of row or round counts as first double crochet and chain-1 unless otherwise stated.

Chain-6 at beginning of row or round counts as first double crochet and chain-3 unless otherwise stated.

SPECIAL STITCH

Decrease (dec): Holding back last lp of each st on hook, tr in next st, [sk next ch, tr in next st] twice, yo, pull through all lps on hook

INSTRUCTIONS

Foundation ch: Ch multiple of 6 plus 12.

Row 1 (RS): Tr dec *(see Stitch Guide)* beg in 8th ch from hook and in next 2 chs, *ch 3, sk next ch, dc in next ch**, ch 3, sk next ch, tr dec in next 3 chs, rep from * across, ending last rep at **, turn.

Row 2: Ch 1, sc in first st, [ch 7, sk next 2 ch sps and next st, sc in next dc] across to last ch sp, ch 7, sk last ch sp, sc in 4th ch of beg 8 chs on row 1, turn.

Rows 3 & 4: Ch 1, sc in first st, [ch 7, sk next ch sp, sc in next st] across, turn.

Row 5: Ch 4 *(see Pattern Notes)*, *work over ch-7 sps of last 3 rows, (tr, {ch 1, tr} twice) in tr dec in row 1, ch 1, dc in next st**, ch 1, rep from * across, ending last rep at **, turn.

Row 6: Ch 6 *(see Pattern Notes)*, [sk next ch sp, **dec** *(see Special Stitch)*, ch 3, sk next ch sp, dc in next st] across, turn.

Rep rows 2–6 consecutively for pattern to desired length, ending with row 5. At end of last row, fasten off. ▪

Swatch 21

PATTERN NOTES

Made with 1 color.

Chain-4 at beginning of row or round counts as first double crochet and chain-2 unless otherwise stated.

Chain-2 at beginning of row or round counts as first double crochet unless otherwise stated.

Chain-3 at beginning of row or round counts as first double crochet and chain-1 unless otherwise stated.

SPECIAL STITCH

Cluster (cl): Holding back last lp of each st on hook, 3 dc as indicated in instructions, yo, pull through all lps on hook.

INSTRUCTIONS

Foundation ch: Ch multiple of 20 plus 24.

Row 1 (RS): Sc in 6th ch from hook (*first 5 chs count as ch-1, dc and ch-2*), ch 5, sk next 3 chs, sc in next ch, ch 1, sk next 3 chs, (**cl**—*see Special Stitch*, ch 1) 3 times in next ch, *sk next 3 chs, sc in next ch, [ch 5, sk next 3 chs, sc in next ch] 3 times, ch 1, sk next 3 chs, (cl, ch 1) 3 times in next ch, rep from * across to last 10 chs, sk next 3 chs, sc in next ch, ch 5, sk next 3 chs, sc in next ch, ch 2, sk next ch, dc in last ch, turn.

Row 2: Ch 1, sc in first dc, ch 5, sk next ch-2 sp, sc in next ch-5 sp, ch 1, sk next sc, [cl in next ch-1 sp, ch 1] 4 times, *sc in next ch-5 sp, [ch 5, sc in next ch-5 sp] twice, ch 1, sk next sc, [cl in next ch-1 sp, ch 1] 4 times, rep from * across to last ch-5 sp, sc in last ch-5 sp, ch 5, sk next 2 chs of beg 5 chs, sc in next ch, turn.

Row 3: Ch 4 (*see Pattern Notes*), sc in next ch-5 sp, ch 1, sk next sc, [cl in next ch-1 sp, ch 1] 5 times, *sc in next ch-5 sp, ch 5, sc in next ch-5 sp, ch 1, sk next sc, [cl in next ch-1 sp, ch 1] 5 times, rep from * to last ch-5 sp, sc in last ch-5 sp, ch 2, dc in last sc, turn.

Row 4: Ch 1, sc in first dc, ch 2, sk next sc, [cl in next ch-1 sp, ch 2] 6 times, *sc in next ch-5 sp, ch 2, sk next sc, [cl in next ch-1 sp, ch 2] 6 times, rep from * to turning ch-4, sk next 2 chs of turning ch, sc in next ch, turn.

Row 5: Ch 4, sk next ch-2 sp, sc in next ch-2 sp, [ch 5, sc in next ch-2 sp] 4 times, *ch 1, sk next ch-2 sp, (dc, ch 1) twice in next sc, sk next ch-2 sp, sc in next ch-2 sp, [ch 5, sc in next ch-2 sp] 4 times, rep from * across to last ch-2 sp, ch 2, sk last ch-2 sp, dc in last sc, turn.

Row 6: Ch 2 (*see Pattern Notes*), (dc, ch 1, cl) in same st as beg ch-2, ch 1, sk next ch-2 sp, sc in next ch-5 sp, [ch 5, sc in next ch-5 sp] 3 times, *ch 1, sk next ch-1 sp, (cl, ch 1) 3 times in next ch-1 sp, sk next ch-1 sp, sc in next ch-5 sp, [ch 5, sc in next ch-5 sp] 3 times, rep from * across to turning ch-4, ch 1, sk next 2 chs of turning ch, (cl, ch 1, 2 dc) in next ch, turn.

Row 7: Ch 2, [cl in next ch-1 sp, ch 1] twice, sc in next ch-5 sp, [ch 5, sc in next ch-5 sp] twice, *ch 1, sk next sc, [cl in next ch-1 sp, ch 1] 4 times, sc in next ch-5 sp, [ch 5, sc in next ch-5 sp] twice, rep from * across to last sc, sk last sc, [ch 1, cl in next ch-1 sp] twice, dc in 2nd ch of turning ch-2, turn.

Row 8: Ch 2, dc in same st as beg ch-2, ch 1, [cl in next ch-1 sp, ch 1] twice, sc in next ch-5 sp, ch 5, sc in next ch-5 sp, *ch 1, sk next sc, [cl in next ch-1 sp, ch 1] 5 times, sc in next ch-5 sp, ch 5, sc in next ch-5 sp, rep from * across to last 2 cls, ch 1, [cl in next ch-1 sp, ch 1] twice, 2 dc in 2nd ch of turning ch-2, turn.

Row 9: Ch 3 (*see Pattern Notes*), [cl in next ch-1 sp, ch 2] 3 times, sc in next ch-5 sp, *ch 2, [cl in next ch-1 sp, ch 2] 6 times, sc in next ch-5 sp, rep from * across to last 2 cls, [ch 2, cl in next ch-1 sp] 3 times, ch 1, dc in 2nd ch of turning ch-2, turn.

Row 10: Ch 1, sc in first dc, ch 5, sk next ch-1 sp, sc in next ch-2 sp, ch 5, sc in next ch-2 sp, ch 1, sk next ch-2 sp, (dc, ch 1) twice in next sc, *sk next ch-2 sp, sc in next ch-2 sp, [ch 5, sc in next ch-2 sp] 4 times, ch 1, sk next ch-2 sp, (dc, ch 1) twice in next sc, rep from * across to last 3 cls, sk next ch-2 sp, [sc in next ch-2 sp, ch 5] twice, sk next cl and next ch of turning ch-3, sc in next ch, turn.

Row 11: Ch 4, sc in next ch-5 sp, ch 5, sc in next ch-5 sp, ch 1, sk next ch-1 sp, (cl, ch 1) 3 times in next ch-1 sp, *sk next ch-1 sp, sc in next ch-5 sp, [ch 5, sc in next ch-5 sp] 3 times, ch 1, sk next ch-1 sp, (cl, ch 1) 3 times in next ch-1 sp, rep from * across to last 2 ch-5 sps, sc in next ch-5 sp, ch 5, sc in next ch-5 sp, ch 2, dc in next sc, turn.

Row 12: Ch 1, sc in first dc, ch 5, sk next ch-2 sp, sc in next ch-5 sp, ch 1, sk next sc, [cl in next ch-1 sp, ch 1] 4 times, *sc in next ch-5 sp, [ch 5, sc in next ch-5 sp] twice, ch 1, sk next sc, [cl in next ch-1 sp, ch 1] 4 times, rep from * across to last ch-5 sp, sc in last ch-5 sp, ch 5, sk next 2 chs of turning ch-4, sc in next ch, turn.

Rep rows 3–12 consecutively for pattern to desired length, ending with row 4. At end of last row, fasten off. ▪

Swatch 22

PATTERN NOTE
Made with 1 color.

SPECIAL STITCH
Decrease (dec): Holding back last lp of each st on hook, dtr in next lp and next sc, yo, pull through all lps on hook.

INSTRUCTIONS
Foundation ch: Ch multiple of 6 plus 2.

Row 1 (RS): Sc in 2nd ch from hook, [ch 6, sc in 2nd ch from hook, hdc in next ch, dc in next ch, tr in next ch, dtr in next ch, sk next 5 chs, sc in next ch] across, turn.

Row 2 (RS): Ch 6, [working in unworked lps of next 6 chs of previous row, sc in next 2 lps, hdc in next lp, dc in next lp, tr in next lp, dtr in next lp] across to last unused lp of last ch-6, **dec** (*see Special Stitch*) in last unused lp and last sc, turn.

Row 3: Ch 1, sc in next dec, [ch 6, sc in 2nd ch from hook, hdc in next ch, dc in next ch,

tr in next ch, dtr in next ch, sc in next dtr (*on previous row*)] across to turning ch, sc in 6th ch of turning ch-6, turn.

Rep rows 2 and 3 alternately for pattern to desired length. At end of last row, fasten off. ▪

Swatch 23

PATTERN NOTES
Made with 1 color.

Chain-3 at beginning of row or round counts as first double crochet unless otherwise stated.

SPECIAL STITCH
Diamond: Dc as indicated in instructions, ch 3, 3 fpdc around last dc made.

INSTRUCTIONS
Foundation ch: Ch multiple of 8 plus 5.

Row 1 (RS): Dc in 4th ch from hook (*first 3 chs count as first dc*), dc in next ch, [sk next 2 chs, **diamond** (*see Special Stitch*) in next ch, sk next 2 chs, dc in each of next 3 chs] across, turn.

Row 2: Ch 3 (*see Pattern Notes*), dc in each of next 2 sts, [ch 2, sc in upper corner of diamond, ch 2, dc in each of next 3 sts] across, turn.

Row 3: Ch 3, dc in each of next 2 sts, [sk next ch-2 sp, diamond in next sc, sk next ch-2 sp, dc in each of next 3 dc] across, turn.

Rep rows 2 and 3 alternately for pattern to desired length, ending with row 2. At end of last row, fasten off. ▪

Swatch 24

PATTERN NOTES
Made with 1 color.

Chain-2 at beginning of row or round counts as first double crochet unless otherwise stated.

SPECIAL STITCH
Circle: Fpdc *(see Stitch Guide)* around next dc, ch 3, (fpdc, ch 3) 5 times around same dc as last fpdc, turn piece upside down, (fpdc, ch 3) 5 times around previous dc on same row, dc around same dc as last fpdc. When completing row, work behind circle in same dc as post worked for beg of circle.

INSTRUCTIONS
Foundation ch: Ch multiple of 12 plus 1.

Row 1 (WS): Dc in 3rd ch from hook *(first 2 chs count as first dc)*, dc in each ch across, turn.

Row 2 (RS): **Ch 2** *(see Pattern Notes)*, dc in each dc across, turn.

Row 3: Ch 2, dc in each dc across, turn.

Row 4: Ch 2, dc in each of next 5 dc, **circle** *(see Special Stitch),* [dc behind same dc as beg of circle and in each of next 11 dc, circle] across to last 6 sts; dc in each of last 6 sts, turn.

Row 5: Ch 2, dc in each of next 5 dc, sk next circle, [dc in each of next 12 dc, sk next circle] across to last 6 sts, dc in last 6 sts, turn.

Rows 6 & 7: Rep row 3.

Row 8: Ch 2, dc in each of next 11 dc, circle, [dc behind same dc as beg of circle and in each of next 11 dc, circle] across to last 12 sts, dc in each of last 12 sts, turn.

Row 9: Ch 2, dc in each of next 11 dc, sk next circle, [dc in each of next 12 dc, sk next circle] across to last 12 sts; dc in each of last 12 sts, turn.

Rows 10 & 11: Rep row 3.

Rep rows 4–11 consecutively for pattern to desired length, ending with row 5. At end of last row, fasten off. ▪

Swatch 25

PATTERN NOTE
Made with 3 colors.

INSTRUCTIONS
Foundation ch: With first color, ch multiple of 8 plus 10.

Row 1 (WS): Hdc in 3rd ch from hook (*first 2 chs count as first hdc*), hdc in each ch across, **changing color** (*see Stitch Guide*) to 2nd color in last st, turn. Fasten off first color.

Row 2 (RS): Ch 1, sc in first hdc, [hdc in next hdc, dc in next hdc, tr in next hdc, 3 dtr in next hdc, tr in next hdc, dc in next hdc, hdc in next hdc, sc in next hdc] across to last 8 sts, hdc in next hdc, dc in next hdc, tr in next hdc, 3 dtr in next hdc, tr in next hdc, dc in next hdc, hdc in next hdc, sc in 2nd ch of beg 2 chs, changing color to 3rd color in last st, turn. Fasten off 2nd color.

Row 3: Ch 2, sk next st, dc in each of next 3 sts, [3 dc in next dtr, dc in each of next 3 sts, **dc dec** (*see Stitch Guide*) in next 3 sts, dc in each of next 3 sts] across to last 6 sts, 3 dc in next dtr, dc in each of next 3 sts, sk next hdc, dc in last sc, changing to 2nd color in last st, turn. Fasten off 3rd color.

Row 4: Ch 3, sk next dc, tr in next dc, dc in next dc, hdc in next dc, [sc in next dc, hdc in next dc, dc in next dc, tr in next dc, **dtr dec** (*see Stitch Guide*) in next 3 sts, tr in next dc, dc in next dc, hdc in next dc] across to last 5 dc, sc in next dc, hdc in next dc, dc in next dc, tr in next dc, sk next dc, tr in 2nd ch of turning ch-2, changing color to first color, turn. Fasten off 3rd color.

Row 5: Ch 2, hdc in each st across and in 3rd ch of turning ch-3, changing color to 2nd color in last st, turn. Fasten off first color.

Row 6: Ch 1, sc in first hdc, [hdc in next hdc, dc in next hdc, tr in next hdc, 3 dtr in next hdc, tr in next hdc, dc in next hdc, hdc in next hdc, sc in next hdc] across to last 7 hdc, hdc in next hdc, dc in next hdc, tr in next hdc, 3 dtr in next hdc, tr in next hdc, dc in next hdc, hdc in next hdc, sc in 2nd ch of turning ch-2, changing to 3rd color in last st, turn. Fasten off 2nd color.

Rep rows 3–6 consecutively for pattern to desired length, ending with row 5. At end of last row, fasten off. ▪

Swatch 28

PATTERN NOTES
Made with 1 color.

Chain-3 at beginning of row or round counts as first double crochet unless otherwise stated.

SPECIAL STITCHES
Cluster (cl): Holding back last lp of each st on hook, 3 dc as indicated in instructions, yo, pull through all lps on hook.

Shell: 5 dc as indicated in instructions.

End shell: 4 dc in ch-1 sp, **dc dec** (*see Stitch Guide*) in same ch sp and 3rd ch of turning ch-3.

Picot: Ch 4, sl st in 4th ch from hook, ch 1.

INSTRUCTIONS
Foundation ch: Ch multiple of 5 plus 9.

Row 1 (RS): Cl (*see Special Stitches*) in 4th ch from hook, *picot (*see Special Stitches*), sk next 4 chs**, (cl, ch 1, cl) in next ch, rep from * across, ending last rep at **, turn.

Row 2: Ch 3 (*see Pattern Notes*), 2 dc in same st, **shell** (*see Special Stitches*) in each ch-1 sp across, ending with 3 dc in last st, turn.

Row 3: Ch 3, (cl, ch 1, cl) in sp between dc group and next shell, *picot, (cl, ch 1, cl) in sp between next 2 shells, rep from * across to last shell and dc group, picot, (cl, ch 1, cl) in sp between last shell and dc group, dc in last st, turn.

Row 4: Ch 3, shell in each ch-1 sp across to last ch-1 sp, **end shell** (*see Special Stitches*) in last ch-1 sp, turn.

Row 5: Ch 3, cl in dc dec, [picot, (cl, ch 1, cl) in sp between next 2 shells] across, ending with picot, (cl, dc) in last st, turn.

Rep rows 2–5 consecutively for pattern to desired length. At end of last row, fasten off. ▪

Swatch 29

PATTERN NOTES

Made with 1 color.

Chain-2 at beginning of row or round counts as first double crochet unless otherwise stated.

Chain-3 at beginning of row or round counts as first double crochet and chain-1 unless otherwise stated.

Chain-4 at beginning of row or round counts as first double crochet and chain-2 unless otherwise stated.

SPECIAL STITCHES

Cluster (cl): Holding last lp of each st on hook, 3 dc as indicated in instructions, yo, pull through all lps on hook.

Decrease (dec): Holding last lp of each st on hook, dc in next dc, sk next cl, dc in next dc, yo, pull through all lps on hook.

INSTRUCTIONS

Foundation ch: Ch multiple of 10 plus 13.

Row 1 (RS): 2 dc in 3rd ch from hook (*first 2 chs count as first dc*), ch 3, sk next 4 chs, sc in next ch, ch 3, sk next 4 chs, [5 dc in next ch, ch 3, sk next 4 chs, sc in next ch, ch 3, sk next 4 chs,] across to last ch, 3 dc in last ch, turn.

Row 2: Ch 3 (*see Pattern Notes*), [dc in next dc, ch 1] twice, **cl** (*see Special Stitches*) in next sc, ch 1, *[dc in next dc, ch 1] 5 times, cl in next sc, ch 1, rep from * across to last 3 sts, [dc in next dc, ch 1] twice, dc in 2nd ch of beg 2 chs, turn.

Row 3: Ch 4 (*see Pattern Notes*), dc in next dc, ch 2, **dec** (*see Special Stitches*), ch 2, *[dc in next dc, ch 2] 3 times, dec, ch 2, rep from * across to last dc, dc in last dc, ch 2, sk next ch of turning ch-3, dc in next ch, turn.

Row 4: Ch 1, sc in first dc, ch 1, [sc in next ch-2 sp, ch 3] across to turning ch-4, sc in next ch of turning ch, ch 1, sk next ch, sc in next ch, turn.

Row 5: Ch 2 (*see Pattern Notes*), 2 dc in same sc as beg ch-2, ch 3, sk next ch-3 sp, sc in next ch-3 sp, ch 3, sk next ch-3 sp, [5 dc in next ch-3 sp, ch 3, sk next ch-3 sp, sc in next ch-3 sp, ch 3, sk next ch-3 sp] across to last 2 sc, sk next sc, 3 dc in last sc, turn.

Rep rows 2–5 consecutively for pattern to desired length, ending with row 3. At end of last row, fasten off. ▪

Swatch 32

PATTERN NOTE
Made with 1 color.

SPECIAL STITCH
Picot: Ch 3, sl st in 3rd ch from hook.

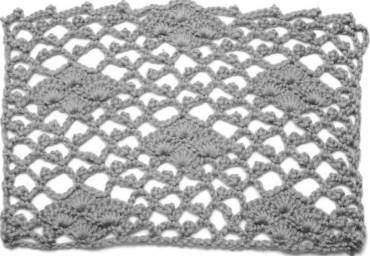

INSTRUCTIONS
Foundation ch: Ch multiple of 24 plus 18.

Row 1 (WS): Sc in 2nd ch from hook, **picot** (see Special Stitch), ch 5, sk next 3 chs, sc in next ch, picot, [ch 5, sk next 3 chs, sc in next ch, ch 5, sk next 3 chs, sc in next ch, picot] across to last 4 chs, ch 5, sk next 3 chs, sc in last ch, turn.

Row 2 (RS): Ch 5, sc in next ch-5 sp, picot, ch 5, sc in next ch-5 sp, 6 dc in next sc, sc in next ch-5 sp, *[ch 5, sc in next ch-5 sp, picot] 4 times, ch 5, sc in next ch-5 sp, 6 dc in next sc, sc in next ch-5 sp, rep from * across to last ch-5 sp, ch 5, sc in last ch-5 sp, picot, ch 2, dc in last sc, turn.

Row 3: Ch 1, sc in next dc, ch 5, sc in next ch-5 sp, 6 dc in next sc, sk next 2 dc, sc in sp between next 2 dc, 6 dc in next sc, sc in next ch-5 sp, ch 5, *[sc in next ch-5 sp, picot, ch 5] 3 times, sc in next ch-5 sp, 6 dc in next sc, sk next 2 dc, sc in sp between next 2 dc, 6 dc in next sc, sc in next ch-5 sp, ch 5, rep from * across to turning ch sp, sc in sp, turn.

Row 4: Ch 5, sc in next ch-5 sp, picot, ch 5, sk next 2 dc, sc in sp between next 2 dc, 6 dc in next sc, sk next 2 dc, sc in sp between next 2 dc, ch 5, *[sc in next ch-5 sp, picot, ch 5] 4 times, sk next 2 dc, sc in sp between next 2 dc, 6 dc in next sc, sk next 2 dc, sc in sp between next 2 dc, ch 5, rep from * across to last ch-5 sp, sc in last ch-5 sp, picot, ch 2, dc in last sc, turn.

Row 5: Ch 1, sc in next dc, ch 5, sc in next ch-5 sp, picot, ch 5, sk next 2 dc, sc in sp between next 2 dc, picot, ch 5, *[sc in next ch-5 sp, picot, ch 5] twice, sc in next ch-5 sp, [ch 5, sc in next ch-5 sp, picot] twice, ch 5, sk next 2 dc, sc in sp

between next 2 dc, picot, ch 5, rep from * across to last ch-5 sp, sc in last ch-5 sp, picot, ch 5, sc in turning ch lp, turn.

Row 6: Ch 5, [sc in next ch-5 sp, picot, ch 5] 4 times, *sc in next ch-5 sp, 6 dc in next sc, sc in next ch-5 sp, [ch 5, sc in next ch-5 sp, picot] 4 times, ch 5, rep from * across to last sc, ch 2, dc in last sc, turn.

Row 7: Ch 1, sc in next dc, ch 5, [sc in next ch-5 sp, picot, ch 5] 3 times, *sc in next ch-5 sp, 6 dc in next sc, sk next 2 dc, sc in sp between next 2 dc, 6 dc in next sc, sc in next ch-5 sp, [ch 5, sc in next ch-5 sp, picot] 3 times, ch 5, rep from * across to turning ch lp, sc in lp, turn.

Row 8: Ch 5, [sc in next ch-5 sp, picot, ch 5] 4 times, *sk next 2 dc, sc in sp between next 2 dc, 6 dc in next sc, sk next 2 dc, sc in sp between next 2 dc**, [ch 5, sc in next ch-5 sp, picot] 4 times, ch 5, rep from * across, ending last rep at **, ch 5, sc in next ch-5 sp, picot ch 2, dc in last sc, turn.

Row 9: Ch 1, sc in first dc, ch 5, sc in next ch-5 sp, picot, ch 5, sc in next ch-5 sp, *[ch 5, sc in next ch-5 sp, picot] twice, ch 5, sk next 2 dc, sc in sp between next 2 dc, picot, [ch 5, sc in next ch-5 sp, picot] twice, ch 5, sc in next ch-5 sp, rep from * across to turning ch lp, ch 5, sc in lp, turn.

Rep rows 2–9 consecutively for pattern to desired length. At end of last row, fasten off. ▪

Swatch 33

PATTERN NOTES

Made with 1 color.

Chain-2 at beginning of row or round counts as first double crochet unless otherwise stated.

INSTRUCTIONS

Foundation ch: Ch multiple of 6 plus 3.

Row 1 (WS): Dc in 3rd ch from hook (*first 2 chs count as first dc*), dc in each ch across, turn.

Row 2 (RS): Ch 2 (*see Pattern Notes*), dc in next dc, [sk next 2 dc, tr in each of next 2 dc, working behind 2 tr just made, tr in each of 2 dc just sk, dc in each of next 2 dc] across, working last dc in 2nd ch of beg 2 chs, turn.

Row 3: Ch 2, dc in next dc, [sk next 2 tr, tr in each of next 2 tr, working in front of 2 tr just made, tr in each of 2 tr just sk, dc in each of next 2 dc] across, working last dc in 2nd ch of turning ch-2, turn.

Row 4: Ch 2, dc in next dc, [sk next 2 tr, tr in each of next 2 tr, working behind 2 tr just made,

tr in each of 2 tr just sk, dc in each of next 2 dc] across, working last dc in 2nd ch of turning ch-2, turn.

Rep rows 3 and 4 alternately for pattern to desired length.

Last row: Ch 2, dc in next dc and in each tr and dc across, working last dc in 2nd ch of turning ch-2. Fasten off. ▪

Swatch 34

PATTERN NOTE
Made with 1 color.

SPECIAL STITCH
Popcorn (pc): 5 dc as indicated in instructions, drop lp from hook, insert hook in first dc of dc group, pull dropped lp through, ch 1 to close.

INSTRUCTIONS
Foundation ch: Ch multiple of 6 plus 12.

Row 1 (WS): Sc in 7th ch from hook, [ch 3, sk next 2 chs, sc in next ch] across to last 2 chs, ch 2, sk next ch, hdc in last ch, forming last ch sp, turn.

Row 2 (RS): Ch 1, sc in first hdc, ch 3, **pc** (*see Special Stitch*) in next ch sp just formed, [ch 3, sc in next ch-3 sp, ch 3, pc in next ch-3 sp] across to beg 6 chs, ch 3, sc in 4th ch of beg 6 chs, turn.

Row 3: Ch 4, [sc in next ch-3 sp, ch 3] across to last ch-3 sp, sc in last ch-3 sp, ch 1, dc in last sc, turn.

Row 4: Ch 1, sc in next dc, [ch 3, sc in next ch-3 sp] across to turning ch, sc in 3rd ch of turning ch-4, turn.

Row 5: Ch 4, [sc in next ch-3 sp, ch 3] across to last ch-3 sp, sc in last ch-3 sp, ch 1, dc in last sc, turn.

Row 6: Ch 6, sc in next ch-3 sp, ch 3, [pc in next ch-3 sp, ch 3, sc in next ch-3 sp, ch 3] across to turning ch, dc in 3rd ch of turning ch-4, turn.

Row 7: Ch 3, [sc in next ch-3 sp, ch 3] across to turning ch lp, sc in lp, ch 1, hdc in 3rd ch of turning ch-6, turn.

Row 8: Ch 1, sc in first hdc, [ch 3, sc in next ch-3 sp] across to turning ch, sc in 2nd ch of turning ch-3, turn.

Row 9: Ch 4, [sc in next ch-3 sp, ch 3] across to last ch-3 sp, sc in last ch-3 sp, ch 1, dc in last sc, turn.

Row 10: Ch 1, sc in first dc, ch 3, pc in next ch-3 sp, [ch 3, sc in next ch-3 sp, ch 3, pc in next ch-3 sp] across to turning ch, sc in 3rd ch of turning ch-4, turn.

Rep rows 3–10 consecutively for pattern to desired length. At end of last row, fasten off. ▪

Swatch 35

PATTERN NOTES

Made with 1 color.

Chain-3 at beginning of row or round counts as first double crochet unless otherwise stated.

Chain-4 at beginning of row or round counts as first double crochet and chain-1 unless otherwise stated.

SPECIAL STITCH

Popcorn (pc): 4 dc as indicated in instructions, drop lp from hook, insert hook in first dc of dc group, pull dropped lp through, ch 1 to close.

INSTRUCTIONS

Foundation ch: Ch multiple of 8 plus 9.

Row 1 (WS): Dc in 4th ch from hook (*first 3 chs count as first dc*) dc in each of next 5 chs, [ch 1, sk next ch, dc in each of next 7 chs] across, turn.

Row 2 (RS): Ch 3 (*see Pattern Notes*), dc in each of next 2 dc, **pc** (*see Special Stitch*) in next dc, dc in each of next 3 dc, [ch 1, dc in each of next 3 dc, pc in next dc, dc in each of next 3 dc] across, turn.

Row 3: Ch 3, dc in each of next 2 dc, *dc in next pc, dc in each of next 3 dc**, ch 1, dc in each of next 3 dc, rep from * across, ending last rep at **, turn.

Row 4: **Ch 4** (*see Pattern Notes*), sk next st, dc in next st, [ch 1, sk next st or ch sp, dc in next st] across, turn.

Row 5: Ch 3, *[dc in next ch sp, dc in next st] 3 times**, ch 1, sk next ch sp, dc in next st, rep from * across, ending last rep at **, turn.

Rep rows 2–5 consecutively for pattern to desired length. At end of last row, fasten off. ▪

Swatch 36

PATTERN NOTE
Made with 1 color.

SPECIAL STITCH
Decrease (dec): Holding back last lp of each st on hook, sc in next 3 chs, sk next sc dec, sc in next 3 chs, yo, pull through all lps on hook.

INSTRUCTIONS
Foundation ch: Ch multiple of 24 plus 27.

Row 1 (RS): Sc dec *(see Stitch Guide)* in 3rd ch from hook and in next 2 chs, [ch 3, sc dec in next 3 chs] 3 times, ch 6, [sc dec in next 3 chs, ch 3] 3 times, *sc dec in next 6 chs, [ch 3, sc dec in next 3 chs] 3 times, ch 6, [sc dec in next 3 sts, ch 3] 3 times, rep from * across to last 4 chs, sc dec in next 3 chs, hdc in last ch, turn.

Row 2: Ch 2, sk first sc dec, [sc dec in next 3 chs, ch 3, sk next cl] 3 times, sc dec in next 3 chs of next ch-6 sp, ch 6, sc dec in next 3 chs of same ch-6 sp, ch 3, [sk next sc dec, sc dec in next 3 chs, ch 3] twice, *dec *(see Special Stitch)*, ch 3, [sk next sc dec, sc dec in next 3 chs, ch 3] twice, sc dec in next 3 chs of next ch-6 sp, ch 6, sc dec in next 3 chs of same ch-6 sp, [ch 3, sk next sc dec, sc dec in next 3 chs] twice, rep from * across to last 2 sc dec, ch 3, sk next sc dec, sc dec in next 3 chs, sk last sc dec, hdc in 2nd ch of beg 2 chs, turn.

Row 3: Ch 2, sk first sc dec, [sc dec in next 3 chs, ch 3, sk next sc dec] 3 times, sc dec in next 3 chs of next ch-6 sp, ch 6, sc dec in next 3 chs of same ch-6 sp, ch 3, [sk next sc dec, sc dec in next 3 chs, ch 3] twice, *dec, ch 3, [sk next sc dec, sc dec in next 3 chs, ch 3] twice, sc dec in next 3 chs of next ch-6 sp, ch 6, sc dec in next 3 chs of same ch-6 sp, [ch 3, sk next sc dec, sc dec in next 3 chs] twice, rep from * across to last 2 sc dec, ch 3, sk next sc dec, sc dec in next 3 chs, sk next sc dec, hdc in 2nd ch of turning ch-2, turn.

Rep row 3 for pattern to desired length. At end of last row, fasten off. ▪

Swatch 37

PATTERN NOTE
Made with 1 color.

SPECIAL STITCHES
Popcorn (pc): 5 dc as indicated in instructions, drop lp from hook, insert hook in first dc of dc group, pull dropped lp through.

Decrease (dec): Holding back last lp of each st on hook, dc in next st, sk next 2 sts, dc in next st, yo, pull through all lps on hook.

INSTRUCTIONS
Foundation ch: Ch multiple of 21 plus 20.

Row 1 (WS): Dc in 3rd ch from hook (*first 3 chs count as first dc*) and in each of next 7 chs, [(dc, ch 3, dc) in next ch, dc in each of next 8 chs, **dec** (*see Special Stitches*), dc in each of next 8 chs] across to last 10 chs, (dc, ch 3, dc) in next ch, dc in each of last 9 chs, turn.

Row 2 (RS): Ch 1, sk first dc, sc in each of next 9 dc, [(sc, **pc**—*see Special Stitches*, sc) in next ch-3 sp, sc in each of next 9 dc, sk next dec, sc in each of next 9 dc] across to last ch-3 sp, (sc, pc, sc) in next ch-3 sp, sc in each of next 8 dc, sk next dc, sc in 2nd ch of beg 2 chs, turn.

Row 3: Ch 2, sk first 2 sc, dc in each of next 7 sc, ch 1, sk next sc, [(dc, ch 3, dc) in next pc, ch 1, sk next sc, dc in each of next 7 sc, dec, dc in each of next 7 sc, ch 1, sk next sc] across to last pc, (dc, ch 3, dc) in last pc, ch 1, sk next sc, dc in each of next 7 sc, sk next sc, dc in last sc, turn.

Row 4: Ch 1, sk first st, sc in each of next 7 dc, pc in next ch-1 sp, sc in next dc, 3 sc in next ch-3 sp, sc in next dc, pc in next ch-1 sp, [sc in each of next 7 dc, sk next dec, sc in each of next 7 dc, pc in next ch-1 sp, sc in next dc, 3 sc in next ch-3 sp, sc in next dc, pc in next ch-1 sp] across

to last 7 dc, sc in each of next 6 dc, sk next dc, sc in 2nd ch of turning ch-2, turn.

Row 5: Ch 2, sk first 2 sc, dc in each of next 5 sc, [ch 1, sk next pc, dc in next sc, ch 1, sk next sc, (dc, ch 3, dc) in next sc, ch 1, sk next sc, dc in next sc, ch 1, sk next pc, dc in each of next 5 sc, dec, dc in each of next 5 sc] across to last 2 pc, ch 1, sk next pc, dc in next sc, ch 1, sk next sc, (dc, ch 3, dc), ch 1, sk next sc, dc in next sc, ch 1, sk last pc, dc in each of next 5 sc, sk next sc, dc in last sc, turn.

Row 6: Ch 1, sk first dc, sc in each of next 5 dc, pc in next ch-1 sp, sc in next dc, sc in next ch-1 sp, sc in next dc, 3 sc in next ch-3 sp, sc in next dc, sc in next ch-1 sp, sc in next dc, [pc in next ch-1 sp, sc in each of next 5 dc, sk next dec, sc in each of next 5 dc, pc in next ch-1 sp, sc in next dc, sc in next ch-1 sp, sc in next dc, 3 sc in next ch-3 sp, sc in next dc, sc in next ch-1 sp, sc in next dc] across to last ch-1 sp, pc in last ch-1 sp, sc in each of next 4 sc, sk next sc, sc in 2nd ch of turning ch-2, turn.

Row 7: Ch 2, sk first 2 sc, dc in each of next 3 sc, [ch 1, sk next st, dc in next sc] twice, ch 1, sk next sc, (dc, ch 3, dc) in next sc, [ch 1, sk next sc, dc in next sc] twice, *ch 1, sk next pc, dc in each of next 3 sc, dec, dc in each of next 3 sc, [ch 1, sk next st, dc in next st] twice, ch 1, sk next sc, (dc, ch 3, dc) in next sc, [ch 1, sk next sc, dc in next sc] twice, rep from * across to last pc, ch 1, sk last pc, dc in each of next 3 sc, sk next sc, dc in last sc, turn.

Row 8: Ch 1, sk first dc, sc in each of next 3 dc, pc in next ch-1 sp, [sc in next dc, sc in next ch-1 sp] twice, sc in next dc, *3 sc in next ch-3 sp, [sc in next dc, sc in next ch-1 sp] twice, sc in next dc, pc in next ch-1 sp, sc in each of next 3 dc, sk next dec, sc in each of next 3 dc, pc in next ch-1 sp, [sc in next dc, sc in next ch-1 sp] twice, sc in next dc, rep from * across to last ch-3 sp, 3 sc in last ch-3 sp, [sc in next dc, sc in next ch-1 sp] twice, sc in next dc, pc in next ch-1 sp, sc in next 2 dc, sk next dc, sc in 2nd ch of turning ch-2, turn.

Row 9: Ch 2, sk first 2 sc, dc in next sc, [ch 1, sk next st, dc in next sc] 3 times, ch 1, sk next sc, (dc, ch 3, dc) in next sc, [ch 1, sk next st, dc in next sc] 4 times, *dec, dc in next sc, [ch 1, sk next st, dc in next sc] 3 times, ch 1, sk next sc, (dc, ch 3, dc) in next sc, [ch 1, sk next st, dc in next sc] 4 times, rep from * across to last 2 sc, sk next sc, dc in last sc, turn.

Row 10: Sk first dc, sc in next dc, pc in next ch-1 sp, (sc in next dc and in next ch-1 sp) 3 times, sc in next dc, 3 sc in next ch-3 sp, (sc in next dc and in next ch-1 sp) 3 times, sc in next dc, pc in next ch-1 sp, *sc in next dc, sk next cl, sc in next dc, pc in next ch-1 sp, (sc in next dc and in next ch-1 sp) 3 times, sc in next dc, 3 sc in next ch-3 sp, (sc in next dc and in next ch-1 sp) 3 times, sc in next dc, pc in next ch-1 sp, rep from * to last dc, sk last dc, sc in 2nd ch of turning ch-2, turn.

Row 11: Ch 2, sk first sc and next pc, dc in each of next 8 sc, *(dc, ch 3, dc) in next sc, dc in each of next 8 sc, dec, dc in each of next 8 sc, (dc, ch 3, dc) in next sc, rep from * across to last 10 sts, dc in each of next 8 sc, sk next pc, dc in last sc, turn.

Row 12: Ch 1, sk first dc, sc in each of next 9 dc, *(sc, pc, sc) in next ch-3 sp, sc in each of next 9 dc, sk next dec, sc in each of next 9 dc, rep from * across to last ch-3 sp, (sc, pc, sc) in next ch-3 sp, sc in each of next 8 dc, sk next dc, sc in 2nd ch of turning ch-2, turn.

Rep rows 3–12 consecutively for pattern to desired length. At end of last row, fasten off. ∎

Swatch 38

PATTERN NOTES
Made with 1 color.

Chain-2 at beginning of row or round counts as first half double crochet unless otherwise stated.

INSTRUCTIONS
Foundation ch: Ch multiple of 5 plus 10.

Row 1 (RS): Dc in 4th ch from hook (*first 3 chs count as first dc*), dc in each ch across, turn.

Row 2: Ch 2 (*see Pattern Notes*), **fpdc** (*see Stitch Guide*) around each of next 2 sts, **bpdc** (*see Stitch Guide*) around each of next 2 sts, [fpdc around each of next 3 sts, bpdc around each of next 2 sts] across, ending with fpdc around each of next 2 sts, hdc in last st, turn.

Row 3: Ch 2, bpdc around each of next 2 sts, fpdc around each of next 2 sts, [bpdc around each of next 3 sts, fpdc around each of next 2 sts] across, ending with bpdc around each of next 2 sts, hdc in last st, turn.

Rep rows 2 and 3 alternately for pattern to desired length. At end of last row, fasten off. ∎

Swatch 39

PATTERN NOTE
Made with 3 colors.

SPECIAL STITCH
Pebble stitch (pebble st): Pull up lp as indicated in instructions, ch 3, keeping ch-3 to front of work, yo, pull through 2 lps on hook.

INSTRUCTIONS
Foundation ch: With first color, ch multiple of 9 plus 12.

Row 1 (WS): Sc in 2nd ch from hook and in each of next 4 chs, 3 sc in next ch, [sc in each of next 3 chs, sk next 2 chs, sc in each of next 3 chs, 3 sc in next ch] across to last 5 chs, sc in each of last 5 chs, turn.

Row 2 (RS): Working in **back lps** *(see Stitch Guide)*, **sc dec** *(see Stitch Guide)* in first 2 sc, sc in each of next 4 sc, 3 sc in next sc, [sc in each of next 3 sc, sk next 2 sc, sc in each of next 3 sc, 3 sc in next sc] across to last 6 sc, sc in each of next 4 sc, sc dec in last 2 sc, turn.

Rows 3–5: Rep row 2. At end of last row, **change color** *(see Stitch Guide)* to 2nd color in last st made, turn. Fasten off first color

Row 6: Working through both lps, ch 1, sl st loosely in each sc across, changing color to 3rd color, turn. Fasten off 2nd color

Row 7: Leaving sl st of previous row unworked and working in back lps of row 5, rep row 2, turn.

Row 8: Working through both lps, ch 1, sc dec in first 2 sts, sc in each of next 4 sc, (**pebble st**—*see Special Stitch*, sc, pebble st) in next sc, *sc in each of next 3 sc, sk next 2 sc, sc in each of next 3 sc, (pebble st, sc, pebble st) in next sc, rep from * across to last 6 sc, sc in each of next 4 sc, sc dec in last 2 sc, turn.

Row 9: Ch 1, sc dec in first 2 sc, sc in each of

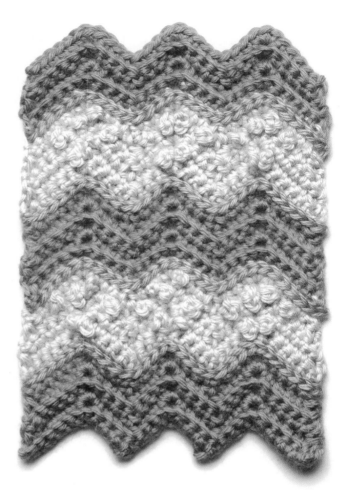

next 4 sts, 3 sc in next st, [sc in each of next 3 sts, sk next 2 sts, sc in each of next 3 sts, 3 sc in next st] across to last 6 sts, sc in each of next 4 sts, sc dec in last 2 sts, turn.

Row 10: Ch 1, sc dec in first 2 sts, sc in each of next 2 sc, pebble st in next sc, sc in next sc, (pebble st, sc, pebble st) in next sc, [sc in next sc, pebble st in next sc, sc in next sc, sk next 2 sc, sc in next sc, pebble st in next sc, sc in next sc, (pebble st, sc, pebble st) in next sc] across to last 6 sc, sc in next sc, pebble st in next sc, sc in next 2 sc, sc dec in last 2 sts, turn.

Row 11: Rep row 9. At end of row, change color to 2nd color in last st, turn. Fasten off 3rd color.

Row 12: Sl st loosely in each sc, change to first color in last st, turn. Fasten off 2nd color.

Row 13: Rep row 7.

Row 14: Working in back lps, ch 1, sc dec in first

2 sts, sc in each of next 4 sc, 3 sc in next sc, [sc in each of next 3 sc, sk next 2 sc, sc in each of next 3 sc, 3 sc in next sc] across to last 6 sc, sc in each of next 4 sc, sc dec in last 2 sc, turn.

Rep rows 3–14 consecutively for pattern to desired length, ending with row 5. At end of last row, fasten off. ▪

Swatch 40

PATTERN NOTES
Made with 2 colors.

Color sequence: 2 rows first color, 2 rows 2nd color, ending with 2 rows first color.

INSTRUCTIONS
Foundation ch: With first color, ch multiple of 4 plus 3.

Row 1 (WS): Sc in 2nd ch from hook, and in each ch across, **changing colors** *(see Stitch Guide)* to 2nd color in last st made, turn. Fasten off first color.

Row 2 (RS): Ch 1, sc in each st across, turn.

Row 3: Ch 1, sc in each st across, changing color to first color in last st, turn. Fasten off 2nd color.

Row 4: Ch 1, sc in each of first 2 sc, on 3rd row below, sk first 2 sc 2 rows below, **fpdc** *(see Stitch Guide)* around each of next 2 sc 2 rows below; sk next 2 sc on this row behind fpdc, sc in next 2 sc, [sk next 2 sc 2 rows below, fpdc around each of next 2 sc 2 rows below, sk next 2 sc on this row behind fpdc, sc in next 2 sc] across, turn.

Row 5: Ch 1, sc in each sc and in each fpdc across, changing to 2nd color in last st, turn. Fasten off first color.

Row 6: Ch 1, sc in each of first 2 sc [fpdc around each of next 2 fpdc 2 rows below, on this row sk next 2 sc behind fpdc, sc in each of next 2 sc] across, turn.

Row 7: Ch 1, sc in each sc and in each fpdc across, changing color to next color in sequence, turn. Fasten off previous color.

Rep rows 6 and 7 alternately for pattern to desired length. At end of last row, fasten off. ▪

Swatch 41

PATTERN NOTE
Made with 1 color.

SPECIAL STITCHES
Cluster (cl): Holding back last lp of each st on hook, 2 dc as indicated in instructions, yo, pull through all lps on hook.

Shell: (Cl, ch 2, cl) as indicated in instructions.

INSTRUCTIONS
Foundation ch: Ch multiple of 20 plus 11.

Row 1 (WS): Cl (see Special Stitches) in 5th ch from hook, sk next 2 chs, **shell** (see Special Stitches) in next ch, *ch 3, sk next 4 chs, sc in next ch, ch 5, sk next 3 chs, sc in next ch, ch 3, sk next 4 chs, [shell in next ch, sk next 2 chs] twice, shell in next ch, rep from * across to last 3 chs, sk next 2 chs, shell in last ch, turn.

Row 2 (RS): Ch 4, cl in next ch-1 sp, shell in ch-2 sp of next shell, [ch 3, 6 dc in next ch-5 sp, ch 3, shell in ch sp of each of next 3 shells] across to ch sp formed by beg 4 chs, cl in ch sp, ch 1, dc in 3rd ch of beg 4 chs, turn.

Row 3: Ch 4, cl in next ch-1 sp, shell in ch sp of next shell, *ch 1, [dc in next dc, ch 1] 6 times, shell in ch sp of each of next 3 shells, rep from * across to turning ch sp, cl in ch sp, ch 1, dc in 3rd ch of beg ch-4, turn.

Row 4: Ch 4, cl in next ch-1 sp, shell in ch sp of next shell, *ch 3, sk next ch-1 sp, [sc in next ch-1 sp, ch 4] 4 times, sc in next ch-1 sp, ch 3, shell in ch sp of each of next 3 shells, rep from * across to turning ch sp, cl in beg ch sp, ch 1, dc in 3rd ch of beg ch-4, turn.

Row 5: Ch 4, cl in next ch-1 sp, shell in ch sp of next shell, *ch 4, [sc in next ch-4 sp, ch 4] 4 times, shell in ch sp of each of next 3 shells, rep from * across to turning ch sp, cl in ch sp, ch 1,

dc in 3rd ch of beg ch-4, turn.

Row 6: Ch 4, cl in next ch-1 sp, shell in ch sp of next shell, *ch 5, sk next ch-4 sp, sc in next ch-4 sp, [ch 4, sc in next ch-4 sp] twice, ch 5, shell in ch sp of each of next 3 shells, rep from * across to turning ch sp, cl in ch sp, ch 1, dc in 3rd ch of beg ch-4, turn.

Row 7: Ch 4, cl in next ch-1 sp, shell in ch sp of next shell, *ch 6, sc in next ch-4 sp, ch 4, sc in next ch-4 sp, ch 6, shell in ch sp of each of next 3 shells, rep from * across to turning ch sp, cl in ch sp, ch 1, dc in 3rd ch of beg ch-4, turn.

Row 8: Ch 4, cl in next ch-1 sp, shell in ch sp of next shell, [ch 7, sc in next ch-4 sp, ch 7, shell in ch sp of each of next 3 shells] across to turning ch sp, cl in ch sp, ch 1, dc in 3rd ch of beg ch-4, turn.

Row 9: Ch 4, cl in next ch-1 sp, shell in ch sp of next shell, [ch 3, sc in next ch-7 sp, ch 5, sc in next ch-7 sp, ch 3, shell in ch sp of each of next 3 shells] across to turning ch sp, cl in ch sp, ch 1, dc in 3rd ch of turning ch-4, turn.

Row 10: Ch 4, cl in next ch-1 sp, shell in ch sp of next shell, [ch 3, 6 dc in next ch-5 sp, ch 3, shell in ch sp of each of next 3 shells] across to turning ch sp, cl in ch sp, ch 1, dc in 3rd ch of beg ch-4, turn.

Rep rows 3–10 consecutively for pattern to desired length. At end of last row, fasten off. ▪

Swatch 42

PATTERN NOTE
Made with 1 color.

INSTRUCTIONS
Foundation ch: Ch multiple of 9 plus 2.

Row 1 (RS): Sc in 2nd ch from hook, [sk next 3 chs, (dc, ch 2, dc) in each of next 2 chs, sk next 3 chs, sc in next ch] across, turn.

Row 2: Ch 1, sc in first sc, [4 dc in each of next 2 ch-2 sps, sc in next sc] across, turn.

Row 3: Ch 7, sk next 3 dc, [sc in each of next 2 dc, ch 7, sk next 7 sts] across to last sc, ch 3, tr in last sc, turn.

Row 4: Ch 1, sc in next tr, [(dc, ch 2, dc) in each of next 2 sc, sc in next ch-7 sp] across to turning ch, sc in 4th ch of turning ch-7, turn.

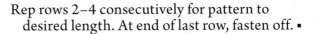

Rep rows 2–4 consecutively for pattern to desired length. At end of last row, fasten off. ▪

Swatch 43

PATTERN NOTE
Made with 1 color.

SPECIAL STITCH
Popcorn (pc): 5 dc as indicated in instructions, drop lp from hook, insert hook in first dc of dc group, pull dropped lp through, ch 1 to close.

INSTRUCTIONS
Foundation ch: Ch multiple of 4 plus 2.

Row 1 (RS): Sc in 2nd ch from hook, [ch 3, **pc** (see Special Stitch) in same ch as last sc, sk next 3 chs, sc in next ch] across, turn.

Row 2: Ch 6, dc in next sc, [ch 3, dc in next sc] across, turn.

Row 3: (Sc, ch 3, pc) in each dc across, sc in 3rd ch of turning ch-6, turn.

Rep rows 2 and 3 alternately for pattern to desired length. At end of last row, fasten off. ▪

Swatch 44

PATTERN NOTE
Made with 2 colors.

INSTRUCTIONS
Foundation ch: With first color, ch multiple of 26 plus 28.

Row 1 (RS): Sc in 2nd ch from hook, [ch 1, sk next ch, sc in next ch] 3 times, ch 1, sk next ch, hdc in next ch, ch 1, sk next ch, dc in next ch, ch 1, sk next ch, *(tr, ch 1) twice in next ch, tr in next ch, ch 1, (tr, ch 1) twice in next ch, sk next ch, dc in next ch, ch 1, sk next ch, hdc in next ch, [ch 1, sk next ch, sc in next ch] 7 times, ch 1, sk next ch, hdc in next ch, ch 1, sk next ch, dc in next ch, ch 1, sk next ch, rep from * across to last 15 chs, (tr, ch 1) twice in next ch, tr in next ch, (tr, ch 1) twice in next ch, sk next ch, dc in next ch, ch 1, sk next ch, hdc in next ch, [ch 1, sk next ch, sc in next ch] 4 times, **changing color** (*see Stitch Guide*) to 2nd color in last st, turn. Fasten off first color.

Row 2: Ch 1, sc in first sc, [ch 1, sk next ch, sc in next st] across, changing color to first color in last st, turn. Fasten off 2nd color.

Row 3: Ch 4, sk next ch, tr in each of next 2 sc, ch 1, sk next ch, dc in next sc, ch 1, sk next ch, hdc in next sc, [ch 1, sk next ch, sc in next sc] 7 times, *ch 1, sk next ch, hdc in next sc, ch 1, sk next ch, dc in next sc, ch 1, sk next ch, tr in each of next 5 sc, ch 1, sk next ch, dc in next sc, ch 1, sk next ch, hdc in next sc, [ch 1, sk next ch, sc in next sc] 7 times, rep from * across to last 5 sc, ch 1, sk next ch, hdc in next sc, ch 1, sk next ch,

dc in next sc, ch 1, sk next ch, tr in each of last 3 sc, changing color to 2nd color in last st, turn. Fasten off first color.

Row 4: Ch 1, sc in first tr, ch 1, sk next tr, sc in next tr, [ch 1, sk next ch, sc in next st] 12 times, *[ch 1, sk next tr, sc in next tr] twice, [ch 1, sk next ch, sc in next st] 12 times, rep from * across to last 2 sts, ch 1, sk last tr, sc in next ch of turning ch-4, changing color to first color in last st, turn. Fasten off 2nd color.

Row 5: Ch 1, sc in first sc, [ch 1, sk next ch, sc in next sc] 3 times, ch 1, sk next ch, hdc in next sc, ch 1, sk next ch, dc in next sc, ch 1, sk next ch, tr in next sc, [ch 1, tr in next ch-1 sp, ch 1, tr in next sc] twice, *ch 1, sk next ch, dc in next sc, ch 1, sk next ch, hdc in next sc, [ch 1, sk next ch, sc in next sc] 7 times, ch 1, sk next ch, hdc in next sc, ch 1, sk next ch, dc in next sc, ch 1, sk next ch, tr in next sc, [ch 1, tr in next ch-1 sp, ch 1, tr in next sc] twice, rep from * across to last 6 sc, ch 1, sk next ch, dc in next sc, ch 1, sk next ch, hdc in next sc, [ch 1, sk next ch, sc in next sc] 4 times, changing color to 2nd color in last st, turn. Fasten off first color.

Rep rows 2–5 consecutively for pattern to desired length, ending with row 3. At end of last row, fasten off. ■

Swatch 45

PATTERN NOTES

Made with 1 color.

Chain-7 at beginning of row counts as first treble crochet and chain-3 unless otherwise stated.

SPECIAL STITCHES

Open shell: (Dc, {ch 1, dc} twice) as indicated in instructions.

Foundation picot: Sc in next ch, ch 3, sc in next ch.

Picot: (Sc, ch 3, sc) as indicated in instructions.

INSTRUCTIONS

Foundation ch: Ch multiple of 7 plus 8.

Row 1 (RS): Sc in 2nd ch from hook, sk next 2 chs, **open shell** (*see Special Stitches*) in next ch, [sk next 2 chs, **foundation picot** (*see Special Stitches*), sk next 2 chs, open shell in next ch] across to last 3 chs, sk next 2 chs, sc in last ch, turn.

Row 2 (WS): **Ch 7** (*see Pattern Notes*), *picot (*see Special Stitches*) in center dc of next open shell, ch 3**, dc in ch sp of next foundation picot, ch

3, rep from * across, ending last rep at **, tr in last st, turn.

Row 3: Ch 1, sc in first st, [open shell in ch sp of next picot, picot in next dc] across, ending with open shell in ch sp of last picot, sc in last st, turn.

Rep rows 2 and 3 alternately for pattern to desired length. At end of last row, fasten off. ▪

Swatch 46

PATTERN NOTES

Made with 2 colors.

Color sequence: First 2 rows first color, then work 1 row with each color beginning with 2nd color.

SPECIAL STITCH

Shell: (Sc, ch 2, sc) as indicated in instructions.

INSTRUCTIONS

Foundation ch: With first color, ch multiple of 34 plus 36.

Row 1 (RS): Sc in 2nd ch from hook, sk next ch, **shell** (see *Special Stitch)* in next ch, [sk next 2 chs, shell in next ch] 4 times, *sk next 2 chs, (shell, ch 3, shell) in next ch, [sk next 2 chs, shell in next ch] 4 times, sk next 2 chs, sc in next ch, sk next 3 chs, sc in next ch, [sk next 2 chs, shell in next ch] 4 times, rep from * to last 20 chs, sk next 2 chs, (shell, ch 3, shell) in next ch, [sk next 2 chs, shell in next ch] 5 times, sk next ch, dc in last ch, turn.

Row 2: Ch 1, sc in first dc and in ch-2 sp of next shell, shell in ch-2 sp of each of next 5 shells, *(shell, ch 3, shell) in next ch-3 sp, shell in ch-2 sp of each of next 4 shells, sc in each of next 2 ch-2 sps, shell in ch-2 sp of each of next 4 shells, rep from * to last ch-3 sp, (shell, ch 3, shell) in last ch-3 sp, shell in ch-2 sp of each of next 5 shells, sc in next ch-2 sp, dc in last sc, **changing color** (see *Stitch Guide)* to next color in last st, turn. Fasten off first color.

Working in **color sequence** (see *Pattern Notes),* rep row 2 for pattern to desired length. At end of last row, fasten off. ▪

Swatch 47

PATTERN NOTES
Made with 1 color.

Chain-2 at beginning of row counts as first double crochet unless otherwise stated.

SPECIAL STITCH
Puff stitch (puff st): Yo, pull up lp as indicated in instructions, [yo, pull up lp in same st] twice, yo, pull through all lps on hook.

INSTRUCTIONS
Foundation ch: Ch multiple of 17 plus 21.

Row 1 (RS): Sc in 2nd ch from hook, sc in each of next 8 chs, [sk next 2 chs, sc in each of next 7 chs, 5 sc in next ch, sc in each of next 7 chs] across to last 11 chs, sk next 2 chs, sc in each of next 8 chs, 2 sc in last ch, turn.

Row 2: Ch 1, 2 sc in first sc, sc in each of next 8 sc, [sk next 2 sc, sc in each of next 8 sc, 3 sc in next sc, sc in each of next 8 sc] across to last 11 sc, sk next 2 sc, sc in each of next 8 sc, 2 sc in last sc, turn.

Row 3: **Ch 2** (see Pattern Notes), dc in same sc as beg ch-2, [ch 1, sk next sc, **puff st** (see Special Stitch) in next sc] 4 times, *sk next 2 sc, [puff st in next sc, ch 1, sk next sc] 8 times, puff st in next sc, rep from * across to last 11 sc, sk next

2 sc, [puff st in next sc, ch 1, sk next sc] 4 times, 2 dc in last sc, turn.

Row 4: Ch 1, 2 sc in first dc, sc in next dc, [sc in next ch-1 sp, sc in next puff st] 3 times, *sc in next ch-1 sp, sk next 2 puff sts, [sc in next ch-1 sp, sc in next puff st] 3 times, sc in next ch-1 sp, 5 sc in next puff st, [sc in next ch-1 sp, sc in next puff st] 3 times, rep from * to last 5 puff sts, sc in next ch-1 sp, sk next 2 puff sts, [sc in next ch-1 sp, sc in next puff st] 3 times, sc in next ch-1 sp, sc in next dc, 2 sc in 2nd ch of turning ch-2, turn.

Rep rows 2–4 consecutively for pattern to desired length. At end of last row, fasten off. ▪

SWATCHES 48–77 DESIGNS BY DARLA SIMS

Swatch 48

PATTERN NOTES

Made with 1 color and 2 hook sizes.

For larger Swatch, work in multiples of any number with repeat of row 2 to desired length and either omit last round or work same amount of single crochet on each side edge with 3 single crochet in each corner.

Join with slip stitch as indicated unless otherwise stated.

INSTRUCTIONS

Row 1: Ch 28 (*see Pattern Notes*), sc in 2nd ch from hook and in each ch across, turn. (*27 sc*)

Rows 2–35: Ch 1, sc in each st across, turn. At end of last row, **do not turn**.

Rnd 36: Working in ends of rows and in sts, with smaller hook, ch 1, evenly sp 25 sc across each edge with 3 sc in each corner, **join** (*see Pattern Notes*) in beg sc. Fasten off. ▪

Swatch 49

PATTERN NOTES

Made with 1 color and 2 hook sizes.

For larger Swatch, work in multiples of chain any number plus 1 with repeat of row 2 to desired length and either omit last round or work same amount of single crochet on each side edge with 3 single crochet in each corner.

Chain-2 at beginning of row or round counts as first half double crochet unless otherwise stated.

Join with slip stitch as indicated unless otherwise stated.

INSTRUCTIONS

Row 1: Ch 28 *(see Pattern Notes)*, hdc in 3rd ch from hook (*first 2 chs count as first hdc*) and in each ch across, turn. *(27 hdc)*

Rows 2–22: Ch 2 *(see Pattern Notes)*, hdc in each st across, turn. At end of last row, **do not turn.**

Rnd 23: Working in ends of rows and in sts, with smaller hook, ch 1, evenly sp 25 sc down each side with 3 sc in each corner, **join** *(see Pattern Notes)* in beg sc. Fasten off. ▪

Swatch 50

PATTERN NOTES

Made with 1 color and 2 hook sizes.

For larger Swatch, work in multiples of chain any number plus 2 with repeat of row 2 to desired length and either omit last round or work same amount of single crochet on each side edge with 3 single crochet in each corner.

Chain-3 at beginning of row or round counts as first double crochet unless otherwise stated.

Join with slip stitch as indicated unless otherwise stated.

INSTRUCTIONS

Row 1: Ch 29 (*see Pattern Notes*), dc in 4th ch from hook (*first 3 chs count as first dc*) and in each ch across, turn. (*27 dc*)

Rows 2–15: Ch 3 (*see Pattern Notes*), dc in each st across, turn. At end of last row, do not turn.

Rnd 16: Working in ends of rows and in sts with smaller hook, ch 1, evenly sp 25 sc down each edge around with 3 sc in each corner, **join** (*see Pattern Notes*) in beg sc. Fasten off. ▪

Swatch 51

PATTERN NOTES

Made with 1 color and 2 hook sizes.

For larger Swatch, work in multiples of chain any number plus 3 with repeat of row 2 to desired length and either omit last round or work same amount of single crochet on each side edge with 3 single crochet in each corner.

Chain-4 at beginning of row or round counts as first treble crochet unless otherwise stated.

Join with slip stitch as indicated unless otherwise stated.

INSTRUCTIONS

Row 1: Ch 30 (see Pattern Notes), tr in 5th ch from hook (*first 4 chs count as first tr*) and in each ch across, turn. (*27 tr*)

Rows 2–9: Ch 4 (see Pattern Notes), tr in each st across, turn. At end of last row, do not turn.

Rnd 10: Working in ends of rows and in sts with smaller hook, ch 1, evenly sp 25 sc down each edge around with 3 sc in each corner, **join** (*see Pattern Notes*) in beg sc. Fasten off. ▪

Swatch 52

PATTERN NOTES
Made with 1 color and 2 hook sizes.

For larger Swatch, work chain in multiples of 6 plus 5 with repeat of rows 2–5 to desired length and either omit last round or work same amount of single crochet on each side edge with 3 single crochet in each corner.

Chain-3 at beginning of row or round counts as first double crochet unless otherwise stated.

Join with slip stitch as indicated unless otherwise stated.

SPECIAL STITCH
Puff stitch (puff st): Yo, insert hook in next st, yo, pull up long lp, [yo, insert hook in same st as last lp, yo, pull up long lp] twice, yo, pull through all lps on hook.

INSTRUCTIONS
Row 1: Ch 29 *(see Pattern Notes)*, dc in 4th ch from hook *(first 3 chs count as first dc)* and in each ch across, turn. *(27 dc)*

Row 2: Ch 3 *(see Pattern Notes)*, **puff st** *(see Special Stitch)* in next st, [ch 3, sk next 2 sts, sc in next st, ch 3, sk next 2 sts, puff st in next st] across to last st, dc in last st, turn. *(2 dc, 4 sc, 5 puff sts, 8 ch sps)*

Row 3: Ch 1, sc in each of first 2 sts, sc in next ch sp, ch 3, [sc in next ch sp, sc in next st, sc in next ch sp, ch 3] 3 times, sc in next ch sp, sc in each of last 2 sts, turn. *(4 ch sps, 15 sc)*

Row 4: Ch 3, dc in each of next 2 sts, [3 dc in next ch sp, dc in each of next 3 sts] across, turn. *(27 dc)*

Row 5: Ch 3, dc in each st across, turn.

Rows 6–16: [Rep rows 2–5 consecutively] 3 times, ending last rep with row 4.

Rnd 17: Working in ends of rows and in sts with smaller hook, ch 1, evenly sp 25 sc down each edge around with 3 sc in each corner, **join** *(see Pattern Notes)* in beg sc. Fasten off. ▪

Swatch 53

PATTERN NOTES

Made with 1 color and 2 hook sizes.

For larger Swatch, work chains in multiples of chain 5 plus 4 with repeat of rows 2 and 3 alternately to desired length and either omit last round or work same amount of single crochet on each side edge with 3 single crochet in each corner.

Chain-3 at beginning of row or round counts as first double crochet unless otherwise stated.

Join with slip stitch as indicated unless otherwise stated.

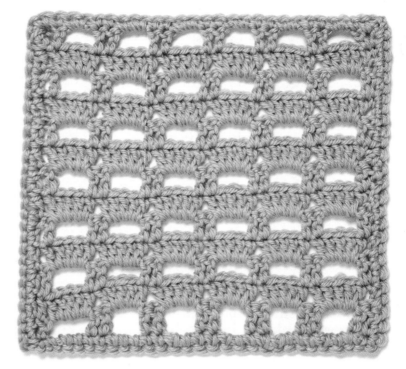

SPECIAL STITCH

Shell: 5 dc as indicated in instructions.

INSTRUCTIONS

Row 1: Ch 34 (see Pattern Notes), dc in 4th ch from hook (first 3 chs count as first dc), [ch 3, sk next 3 chs, dc in each of next 2 chs] across, turn. (6 ch sps, 14 dc)

Row 2: Ch 3 (see Pattern Notes), **shell** (see Special Stitch) in center ch of each ch sp across to last 2 sts, sk next st, dc in last st, turn. (2 dc, 6 shells)

Row 3: Ch 3, [dc in first st of next shell, ch 3, dc in last st of same shell] across, ending with dc in last st, turn.

Rows 4–13: [Rep rows 2 and 3 alternately] 5 times. At end of last row, **do not turn.**

Rnd 14: Working in ends of rows and in sts, with smaller hook, ch 1, evenly sp 25 sc down each edge around with 3 sc in each corner, **join** (see Pattern Notes) in beg sc. Fasten off. ▪

Swatch 54

PATTERN NOTES

Made with 1 color and 2 hook sizes.

For larger Swatch, work chain in multiples of chain 5 plus 8 with repeat of rows 4–7 consecutively to desired length and either omit last round or work same amount of single crochet on each side edge with 3 single crochet in each corner.

Chain-3 at beginning of row or round counts as first double crochet unless otherwise stated.

Join with slip stitch as indicated unless otherwise stated.

INSTRUCTIONS

Row 1: Ch 30 (see Pattern Notes), dc in 4th ch from hook (first 3 chs count as first dc) and in each ch across, turn. (28 dc)

Row 2: Ch 1, sc in each st across, turn.

Row 3: Ch 3 (see Pattern Notes), dc in next st, *sk next 2 sts 2 rows below, **fptr** (see Stitch Guide) around each of next 2 sts 2 rows below, working in front, fptr around first sk st, fptr around 2nd sk st, fptr around each of next 2 sts 2 rows below**, dc in each of next 3 sts, rep from * around, ending last rep at **, dc in each of last 2 sts, turn.

Row 4: Ch 1, sc in each st across, turn.

Row 5: Ch 3, dc in next st, *fptr around each of next 2 post sts, sk next 2 post sts, fptr around each of next 2 post sts, working in front of last 2 post sts, fptr in first sk post st, fptr around

2nd post st**, dc in each of next 3 sts, rep from * across, ending last rep at **, dc in each of last 2 sts, turn.

Row 6: Ch 1, sc in each st across, turn.

Row 7: Ch 3, dc in next st, *sk next 2 post sts, fptr around each of next 2 post sts, working in front of last post st, fptr around first sk st, fptr around 2nd sk st, fptr around each of next 2 post sts**, dc in each of next 3 sts, rep from * across, ending last rep at **, dc in each of last 2 sts, turn.

Rows 8–23: [Rep rows 4–7 consecutively] 4 times. At end of last row, **do not turn**.

Rnd 24: Working in ends of rows and in sts with smaller hook, ch 1, evenly sp 25 sc down each edge around with 3 sc in each corner, **join** (see Pattern Notes) in beg sc. Fasten off. ▪

Swatch 55

PATTERN NOTES

Made with 1 color and 2 hook sizes.

For larger Swatch, work chain in multiples of 18 plus 3 with repeat of rows 2–5 consecutively to desired length and either omit last round or work same amount of single crochet on each side edge with 3 single crochet in each corner.

Chain-3 at beginning of row or round counts as first double crochet unless otherwise stated.

Join with slip stitch as indicated unless otherwise stated.

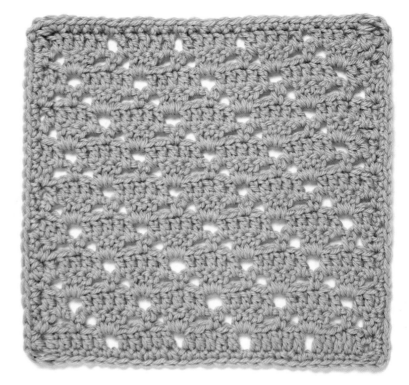

INSTRUCTIONS

Row 1: **Ch 33** (*see Pattern Notes*), dc in 4th ch from hook (*first 3 chs count as first dc*), dc in each of next 4 chs, ch 1, sk next ch, [dc in each of next 5 chs, ch 1, sk next ch] across to last 6 chs, dc in each of last 6 chs, turn. (*4 ch sps, 27 dc*)

Row 2: **Ch 3** (*see Pattern Notes*), dc in same st as beg ch-3, ch 2, sk next 2 sts, sc in next st, ch 2, sk next 2 sts, [3 dc in next ch sp, ch 2, sk next 2 sts, sc in next st, ch 2, sk next 2 sts] across, ending with dc in last st, turn. (*5 sc, 10 ch sps, 16 dc*)

Row 3: Ch 3, dc in next st, dc in next ch sp, ch 1, dc in next ch sp, [dc in each of next 3 sts, dc in next ch sp, ch 1, dc in next ch sp] across, ending with dc in each of last 2 sts, turn. (*5 ch sps, 26 dc*)

Row 4: Ch 1, sc in first st, ch 2, 3 dc in next ch sp, *ch 2, sk next 2 sts**, 3 dc in next ch sp, rep from * across, ending last rep at **, sc in last st, turn. (*6 sc, 10 ch sps, 15 dc*)

Row 5: Ch 3, dc in next ch sp, dc in each of next 3 sts, dc in next ch sp, [ch 1, dc in next ch sp, dc in each of next 3 sts, dc in next ch sp] across, ending with dc in last st, turn. (*4 ch sps, 27 dc*)

Rows 6–17: [Rep rows 2–5 consecutively] 3 times. At end of last row, **do not turn.**

Rnd 18: Working in ends of rows and in sts, with smaller hook, ch 1, evenly sp 25 sc down each edge around with 3 sc in each corner, **join** (*see Pattern Notes*) in beg sc. Fasten off. ▪

Swatch 56

PATTERN NOTES

Made with 1 color and 2 hook sizes.

For larger Swatch, work chain in multiples of 2 plus 4 with repeat of rows 2–5 consecutively to desired length and either omit last round or work same amount of single crochet on each side edge with 3 single crochet in each corner.

Chain-3 at beginning of row or round counts as first double crochet unless otherwise stated.

Chain-2 at beginning of row or round counts as first half double crochet unless otherwise stated.

Join with slip stitch as indicated unless otherwise stated.

SPECIAL STITCHES

Cross-stitch (cross-st): Sk next ch or st, dc in next ch or st, working in front of last dc, dc in sk ch or st.

Beginning star stitch (beg star st): Insert hook in 2nd ch from hook, yo, pull lp through, insert hook in next ch, yo, pull lp through, insert hook in first st of last row, yo, pull lp through, [insert hook in next st of last row, yo, pull lp through] twice, yo, pull through all lps on hook, ch 1 to close and form eye.

Star stitch (star st): Insert hook in eye of last star st, yo, pull lp through, insert hook through last 2 lps on side of last star st, yo, pull lp through, insert hook in same st on last row as last star st, yo, pull lp through, [insert hook in next st of last row, yo, pull lp through] twice, yo, pull through all lps on hook, ch 1 to close and form eye.

INSTRUCTIONS

Row 1: Ch 30 (see Pattern Notes), dc in 5th ch from hook, working in front of dc just made, dc in 4th ch from hook (cross-st made) (first 3 chs count as first dc), **cross-st** (see Special Stitches) across to last ch, dc in last ch, turn (2 dc, 13 cross-sts)

Row 2: Ch 1, sc in each st across, turn. (28 sc)

Row 3: Ch 3 (see Pattern Notes), **beg star st** (see Special Stitches), **star st** (see Special Stitches) across to last st, hdc in last st, turn. (2 hdc, 13 star sts)

Row 4: Ch 2 (see Pattern Notes), 2 hdc in eye of each star st across, hdc in last st, turn. (28 hdc)

Row 5: Ch 3, cross-st across, dc in last st, turn.

Rows 6–17: [Rep rows 2–5 consecutively] 3 times. At end of last row, **do not turn.**

Rnd 18: Working in ends of rows and in sts, with smaller hook, ch 1, evenly sp 25 sc down each edge around with 3 sc in each corner, **join** (see Pattern Notes) in beg sc. Fasten off. ▪

Swatch 57

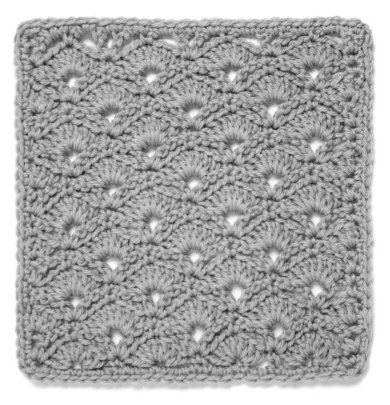

PATTERN NOTES

Made with 1 color and 2 hook sizes.

For larger Swatch, work chain in multiples of 16 plus 2 with repeat of rows 3–6 to desired length and either omit last round or work same amount of single crochet on each side edge with 3 single crochet in each corner.

Chain-3 at beginning of row or round counts as first double crochet unless otherwise stated.

Join with slip stitch as indicated unless otherwise stated.

SPECIAL STITCHES

Shell: 7 dc as indicated in instructions.

V-stitch (V-st): (Dc, ch 2, dc) as indicated in instructions.

INSTRUCTIONS

Row 1: Ch 34 (*see Pattern Notes*), sc in 2nd ch from hook, [sk next 3 chs, **shell** (*see Special Stitches*) in next ch, sk next 3 chs, sc in next ch] across, turn. (*5 sc, 4 shells*)

Row 2: Ch 3 (*see Pattern Notes*), dc in same st as beg ch-3, ch 2, sc in center st of next shell, ch 2, [**V-st** (*see Special Stitches*) in next sc, ch 2, sc in center st of next shell, ch 2] across, 2 dc in last st, turn. (*3 V-sts, 4 sc, 4 dc, 8 ch sps*)

Row 3: Ch 3, 3 dc in same st as beg ch-3, sc in next sc, sk next ch sp, [shell in ch sp of next V-st, sc in next sc, sk next ch sp] across to last 2 sts, sk next st, 4 dc in last st, turn.

Row 4: Ch 1, sc in first st, ch 2, V-st in next sc, ch 2, [sc in center st of next shell, ch 2, V-st in next sc, ch 2] across to last 4 sts, sk next 3 sts, sc in last st, turn. (*4 V-sts, 5 sc, 8 ch sps*)

Row 5: Ch 1, sc in first st, sk next ch sp, shell in ch sp of next V-st, [sc in next sc, sk next ch sp, shell in ch sp of next V-st] across, sc in last st, turn.

Row 6: Ch 3, dc in same st as beg ch-3, ch 2, sc in center st of next shell, ch 2, [V-st in next sc, ch 2, sc in center st of next shell, ch 2] across with 2 dc in last st, turn.

Rows 7–18: [Rep rows 3–6 consecutively] 3 times. At end of last row, **do not turn.**

Rnd 19: Working in ends of rows and in sts with smaller hook, ch 1, evenly sp 25 sc down each edge around with 3 sc in each corner, **join** (*see Pattern Notes*) in beg sc. Fasten off. ▪

Swatch 58

PATTERN NOTES

Made with 1 color and 2 hook sizes.

For larger Swatch, work chain in multiples of 2 plus 4 with repeat of row 3 to desired length and either omit last round or work same amount of single crochet on each side edge with 3 single crochet in each corner.

Join with slip stitch as indicated unless otherwise stated.

INSTRUCTIONS

Row 1: **Ch 28** (*see Pattern Notes*), (sc, dc) (*pattern sts*) in 2nd ch from hook, sk next ch, [(sc, dc) in next ch, sk next ch] across, sc in last ch, turn. (*1 sc, 13 pattern sts*)

Row 2: Ch 1, (sc, dc) in first st, sk next st, [(sc, dc) in next st, sk next st] across, sc in last st, turn.

Rows 3–25: Ch 1, (sc, dc) in first st, sk next st, [(sc, dc) in next st, sk next st] across, sc in last st, turn. At end of last row, **do not turn**.

Rnd 26: Working in ends of rows and in sts, with smaller hook, ch 1, evenly sp 25 sc down each edge around with 3 sc in each corner, **join** (*see Pattern Notes*) in beg sc. Fasten off. ▪

Swatch 59

PATTERN NOTES

Made with 1 color and 2 hook sizes.

For larger Swatch, work chain in multiples of 3 plus 4 with repeat of rows 2–5 consecutively to desired length and either omit last round or work same amount of single crochet on each side edge with 3 single crochet in each corner.

Join with slip stitch as indicated unless otherwise stated.

SPECIAL STITCH

Cluster (cl): Holding back last lp of each st on hook, 3 dc as indicated in instructions, yo, pull through all lps on hook.

INSTRUCTIONS

Row 1: Ch 28 (*see Pattern Notes*), sc in 2nd ch from hook and in each ch across, turn. (*27 sc*)

Row 2: Ch 1, sc in first st, **cl** (*see Special Stitch*) in next st, [sc in each of next 2 sts, cl in next st] across, ending with sc in last st, turn. (*9 cls, 18 sc*)

Row 3: Ch 1, sc in each st across, turn.

Row 4: Ch 1, sc in each of first 2 sts, cl in next st, [sc in each of next 2 sts, cl in next st] across to last 3 sts, sc in each of last 3 sts, turn. (*8 cls, 19 sc*)

Row 5: Ch 1, sc in each st across, turn.

Rows 6–31: [Rep rows 2–5 consecutively] 7 times, ending last rep with row 3. At end of last row, **do not turn.**

Rnd 32: Working in ends of rows and in sts, with smaller hook, ch 1, evenly sp 25 sc down each edge around with 3 sc in each corner, **join** (*see Pattern Notes*) in beg sc. Fasten off. ▪

Swatch 60

PATTERN NOTES

Made with 1 color and 2 hook sizes.

For larger Swatch, work chain in multiples of 4 plus 9 with repeat of rows 3 and 4 alternately to desired length and either omit last round or work same amount of single crochet on each side edge with 3 single crochet in each corner.

Chain-3 at beginning of row or round counts as first double crochet unless otherwise stated.

Join with slip stitch as indicated unless otherwise stated.

SPECIAL STITCH

Crossed long double crochet (crossed long dc): Insert hook in sp after next 4-dc group, yo, pull up long lp, [yo, pull through 2 lps on hook] twice, ch 2, working around st just made, yo, insert hook in sp before same 4-dc group, yo pull up long lp, [yo, pull through 2 lps on hook] twice.

INSTRUCTIONS

Row 1: Ch 37 *(see Pattern Notes)*, 2 dc in 5th ch from hook, 2 dc in next ch, sk next 2 chs, [2 dc in each of next 2 chs, sk next 2 chs] across to last ch, dc in last ch, turn. *(2 dc, 8 4-dc groups)*

Row 2: Ch 3 *(see Pattern Notes)*, **crossed long dc** *(see Special Stitch)* across, dc in top of turning ch, turn. *(8 crossed long dc)*

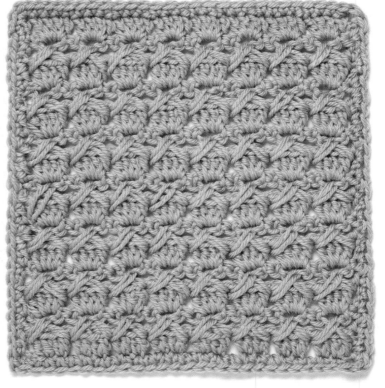

Row 3: Ch 3, 4 dc in each ch sp across, ending with dc in last st, turn.

Row 4: Ch 3, crossed long dc across, dc in last st, turn.

Rows 5–15: [Rep rows 3 and 4 alternately] 6 times, ending last rep with row 3. At end of last row, **do not turn.**

Rnd 16: Working in ends of rows and in sts with smaller hook, ch 1, evenly sp 25 sc down each edge around with 3 sc in each corner, **join** *(see Pattern Notes)* in beg sc. Fasten off. ▪

Swatch 61

PATTERN NOTES

Made with 1 color and 2 hook sizes.

For larger Swatch, work chain in multiples of 6 plus 7 with repeat of rows 2 and 3 alternately to desired length and either omit last round or work same amount of single crochet on each side edge with 3 single crochet in each corner.

Chain-3 at beginning of row or round counts as first double crochet unless otherwise stated.

Chain-4 at beginning of row or round counts as first double crochet and chain-1 unless otherwise stated.

Join with slip stitch as indicated unless otherwise stated.

INSTRUCTIONS

Row 1: Ch 31 *(see Pattern Notes)*, dc in 4th ch from hook *(first 3 chs count as first dc)*, dc in each of next 3 chs, [ch 1, sk next ch, dc in each of next 5 chs] across, turn. *(4 ch sps, 25 dc)*

Row 2: Ch 4 *(see Pattern Notes)*, dc in same st as beg ch-4, sk next 3 sts, (dc, ch 1, dc) in next st, [ch 1, sk next ch sp, (dc, ch 1, dc) in next st, sk next 3 sts, (dc, ch 1, dc) in next st] across, turn. *(14 ch sps, 20 dc)*

Row 3: Ch 3 *(see Pattern Notes)*, dc in next ch sp, sk next st, dc in sp between next 2 sts, sk next st, dc in next ch sp, dc in next st, [ch 1, sk next ch sp, dc in next st, dc in next ch sp, sk next st, dc in sp between next 2 sts, sk next st, dc in next ch sp, dc in next st] across, turn. *(4 ch sps, 25 dc)*

Rows 4–15: [Rep rows 2 and 3 alternately] 6 times. At end of last row, **do not turn.**

Rnd 16: Working in ends of rows and in sts, with smaller hook, ch 1, evenly sp 25 sc down each edge around with 3 sc in each corner, **join** *(see Pattern Notes)* in beg sc. Fasten off. ▪

Swatch 62

PATTERN NOTES

Made with 1 color and 2 hook sizes.

For larger Swatch, work chain in multiples of any even number with repeat of row 2 to desired length and either omit last round or work same amount of single crochet on each side edge with 3 single crochet in each corner.

Join with slip stitch as indicated unless otherwise stated.

SPECIAL STITCH

Kernel stitch (kernel st): Insert hook in same ch or st as last st made, yo, pull lp through, insert hook in next st, yo, pull lp through, yo, pull through all lps on hook.

INSTRUCTIONS

Row 1: Ch 26 (see Pattern Notes), sc in 2nd ch from hook, **kernel st** (see Special Stitch) across, turn. (1 sc, 24 kernel sts)

Rows 2–30: Ch 1, sc in first st, kernel st across, turn. At end of last row, **do not turn.**

Rnd 31: Working in ends of rows and in sts, with smaller hook, ch 1, evenly sp 25 sc down each edge around with 3 sc in each corner, **join** (see Pattern Notes) in beg sc. Fasten off. ▪

Swatch 63

PATTERN NOTES

Made with 1 color and 2 hook sizes.

For larger Swatch, work chain in multiples of 6 plus 7 with repeat of rows 3 and 4 alternately to desired length and either omit last round or work same amount of single crochet on each side edge with 3 single crochet in each corner.

Chain-3 at beginning of row or round counts as first double crochet unless otherwise stated.

Join with slip stitch as indicated unless otherwise stated.

SPECIAL STITCHES

V-stitch (V-st): (Dc, ch 2, dc) as indicated in instructions.

Puff stitch (puff st): Yo, insert hook in next st, yo, pull up long lp, [yo, insert hook in same st, yo, pull up long lp] twice, yo, pull through all lps on hook.

INSTRUCTIONS

Row 1: Ch 31 *(see Pattern Notes)*, **V-st** *(see Special Stitches)* in 5th ch from hook *(first 4 chs count as first dc and ch-1)*, [sk next 2 chs, **puff st** *(see Special Stitches)* in next ch, sk next 2 chs, V-st in next ch] across to last 2 chs, sk next ch, dc in last ch, turn. *(2 dc, 4 puff sts, 5 V-sts)*

Row 2: Ch 3 *(see Pattern Notes)*, puff st in ch sp of next V-st, [V-st in next puff st, puff st in ch sp of next V-st] across, ending with dc in last st, turn. *(2 dc, 4 V-sts, 5 puff sts)*

Row 3: Ch 3, V-st in next puff st, [puff st in ch sp of next V-st, V-st in next puff st] across, ending with dc in last st, turn.

Row 4: Ch 3, puff st in ch sp of next V-st, [V-st in next puff st, puff st in ch sp of next V-st] across, ending with dc in last st, turn.

Rows 5–15: [Rep rows 3 and 4 alternately] 6 times, ending last rep with row 3. At end of last row, **do not turn.**

Rnd 16: Working in ends of rows and in sts with smaller hook, ch 1, evenly sp 25 sc down each edge around with 3 sc in each corner, **join** *(see Pattern Notes)* in beg sc. Fasten off. ▪

Swatch 64

PATTERN NOTES

Made with 1 color and 2 hook sizes.

For larger Swatch, work chain in multiples of 3 plus 5 with repeat of row 2 to desired length and either omit last round or work same amount of single crochet on each side edge with 3 single crochet in each corner.

Join with slip stitch as indicated unless otherwise stated.

SPECIAL STITCH

Pattern stitch (pattern st): (Sc, ch 7, dc) as indicated in instructions.

INSTRUCTIONS

Row 1: Ch 35 (*see Pattern Notes*), sc in 2nd ch from hook, sk next 2 chs, [**pattern st** (*see Special Stitches*) in next ch, sk next 2 chs] across, ending with sc in last ch, turn. (*2 sc, 10 pattern sts*)

Rows 2–22: Ch 1, sc in first st, pattern st in ch sp of each pattern st across, ending with sc in last st, turn.

Rnd 23: Working in ends of rows and in sts, with smaller hook, ch 1, evenly sp 25 sc down each edge around with 3 sc in each corner, **join** (*see Pattern Notes*) in beg sc. Fasten off. ▪

Swatch 65

PATTERN NOTES
Made with 1 color and 2 hook sizes.

Chain-3 at beginning of row or round counts as first double crochet unless otherwise stated.

Join with slip stitch as indicated unless otherwise stated.

SPECIAL STITCH
Shell: (2 dc, ch 1, 2 dc) as indicated in instructions.

INSTRUCTIONS
LARGER SWATCH
Row 1: Ch in multiples of 14 plus 17, **shell** *(see Special Stitch)* in 6th ch from hook *(first 5 chs count as first dc and sk 2 chs)*, *ch 3, sk next 3 chs, sc in next ch, ch 3, sk next 3 chs, shell in next ch, ch 3, sk next 2 chs, dc in next ch**, sk next 2 chs, shell in next ch, ch 3, sk next 3 chs, sc in next ch, ch 3, sk next 3 chs, shell in next ch, sk next 2 chs, rep from * across, ending last rep at **, dc in last ch, turn.

Row 2: Ch 3 *(see Pattern Notes)*, *shell in ch sp of next shell, ch 3, [sc in next ch sp ch 3] twice, shell in ch sp of next shell**, **bpdc** *(see Stitch Guide)* around next dc between shells, rep from * across, ending last rep at **, dc in 5th ch of beg ch-5, turn.

Row 3: Ch 3, *shell in ch sp of next shell, ch 3, sk next ch sp, sc in next ch sp, ch 3, sk next ch sp, shell in ch sp of next shell**, **fpdc** *(see Stitch Guide)* around next post st, rep from * across, ending last rep at **, dc in last st, turn.

Row 4: Ch 3, *shell in ch sp of next shell, ch 3, [sc in next ch sp, ch 3] twice, shell in ch sp of next shell**, bpdc around next post st, rep from * across, ending last rep at **, dc in last st, turn.

Row 5: Ch 3, *shell in ch sp of next shell, ch 3, sk next ch sp, sc in next ch sp, ch 3, sk next ch sp, shell in ch sp of next shell**, fpdc around post

of next st, rep from * across, ending last rep at **, dc in last st, turn.

Next rows: [Rep rows 4 and 5 alternately] to desired length.

Next row: Ch 1, sc in first st, *ch 2, sc in ch sp of next shell, ch 2, [sc in next ch sp, ch 2] twice, sc in ch sp of next shell, ch 2**, bpdc around next post st, rep from * across, ending last rep at **, sc in last st, turn.

Last rnd: Working in sts and in ends of rows, with smaller hook, ch 1, evenly sp sc down each edge around with 3 sc in each corner, **join** *(see Pattern Notes)* in beg sc. Fasten off.

SMALLER SWATCH
Row 1: Ch 31, **shell** *(see Special Stitch)* in 6th ch from hook *(first 5 chs count as first dc and sk 2 chs)*, ch 3, sk next 3 chs, sc in next ch, ch 3, sk next 3 chs, shell in next ch, ch 3, sk next 2 chs, dc in next ch, sk next 2 chs, shell in next ch, ch 3, sk next 3 chs, sc in next ch, ch 3, sk next 3 chs, shell in next ch, sk next 2 chs, dc in last ch, turn. *(2 sc, 3 dc, 4 ch sps, 4 shells)*

Row 2: Ch 3 *(see Pattern Notes)*, *shell in ch sp

of next shell, ch 3, [sc in next ch sp, ch 3] twice, shell in ch sp of next shell*, **bpdc** (*see Stitch Guide*) around next dc between shells, rep between * once, dc in 5th ch of beg ch-5, turn. (*1 bpdc, 2 dc, 4 shells, 6 ch sps*)

Row 3: Ch 3, *shell in ch sp of next shell, ch 3, sk next ch sp, sc in next ch sp, ch 3, sk next ch sp, shell in ch sp of next shell*, **fpdc** (*see Stitch Guide*) around next post st, rep between * once, ending with dc in last st, turn.

Row 4: Ch 3, *shell in ch sp of next shell, ch 3, [sc in next ch sp, ch 3] twice, shell in ch sp of next shell*, bpdc around next post st, rep between * once, dc in last st, turn.

Row 5: Ch 3, *shell in ch sp of next shell, ch 3, sk next ch sp, sc in next ch sp, ch 3, sk next ch sp, shell in ch sp of next shell*, fpdc around post of next st, rep between * once, dc in last st, turn.

Rows 6–13: [Rep rows 4 and 5 alternately] 4 times.

Row 14: Ch 1, sc in first st, *ch 2, sc in ch sp of next shell, ch 2, [sc in next ch sp, ch 2] twice, sc in ch sp of next shell, ch 2*, bpdc around next post st, rep between * once, sc in last st, turn.

Rnd 15: Working in sts and in ends of rows, with smaller hook, ch 1, evenly sp 25 sc down each edge around with 3 sc in each corner, **join** (*see Pattern Notes*) in beg sc. Fasten off. ▪

Swatch 66

PATTERN NOTES

Made with 1 color and 2 hook sizes.

For larger Swatch, work chain in multiples of any even number with repeat of row 2 to desired length and either omit last round or work same amount of single crochet on each side edge with 3 single crochet in each corner.

Chain-2 at beginning of row or round counts as first half double crochet unless otherwise stated.

Join with slip stitch as indicated unless otherwise stated.

INSTRUCTIONS

Row 1: Ch 28 (*see Pattern Notes*), hdc in 3rd ch from hook (*first 2 chs counts as first hdc*), hdc in each ch across, turn. (*27 hdc*)

Rows 2–25: Ch 2 (*see Pattern Notes*), hdc in sp between first 2 sts, [hdc in sp between next 2 sts] across to last 2 sts, sk next st, hdc in last st, turn.

Rnd 26: Working in sts and in ends of rows, with smaller hook, ch 1, evenly sp 25 sc down each edge around with 3 sc in each corner, **join** (*see Pattern Notes*) in beg sc. Fasten off. ▪

Swatch 67

PATTERN NOTES
Made with 1 color and 2 hook sizes.

For larger Swatch, work chain in multiples of 12 plus 4 with repeat of rows 3–8 consecutively to desired length and either omit last round or work same amount of single crochet on each side edge with 3 single crochet in each corner.

Chain-2 at beginning of row or round counts as first half double crochet unless otherwise stated.

Join with slip stitch as indicated unless otherwise stated.

SPECIAL STITCH
Popcorn (pc): Working around st on last row and in top of fptr on row before last, 5 hdc in next st, drop lp from hook, insert hook in first hdc of group, pull dropped lp through.

INSTRUCTIONS
Row 1: Ch 28 *(see Pattern Notes)*, hdc in 3rd ch from hook *(first 2 chs count as first hdc)*, hdc in each ch across, turn. *(27 hdc)*

Row 2: Ch 2 *(see Pattern Notes)*, hdc in each st across, turn.

Row 3: Ch 2, **fptr** *(see Stitch Guide)* around next st on row before last, *sk next st on this row behind fptr just made, hdc in each of next 2 sts on this row, sk next 4 sts on row before last, [fptr around next st on row before last, sk next st on this row behind fptr just made, hdc in each of next 2 sts on this row] 3 times, sk next 4 sts on row before last, fptr around next st, rep from * once, sk next st on this row behind fptr just made, hdc in last st, turn.

Row 4: Ch 2, hdc in each st across, turn.

Row 5: Ch 2, fptr around next post st on row before last, *hdc in each of next 5 sts on this row, **pc** *(see Special Stitch)*, hdc in each of next 5 sts on this row, fptr around next post st on row before last, rep from * once, hdc in last st, turn.

Row 6: Ch 2, hdc in each st across, turn.

Row 7: Ch 2, fptr around next post st on row before last, [hdc in each of next 11 sts on last row, fptr around next post st on row before last] twice, hdc in last st, turn.

Row 8: Ch 2, hdc in each st across, turn.

Rows 9–23: [Rep rows 3–8 consecutively] 3 times, ending last rep with row 5. At end of last row, **do not turn.**

Rnd 24: Working in ends of rows and in sts, with smaller hook, ch 1, evenly sp 25 sc down each edge around with 3 sc in each corner, **join** *(see Pattern Notes)* in beg sc. Fasten off. ▪

Swatch 68

PATTERN NOTES

Made with 1 color and 2 hook sizes.

For larger Swatch, work chain in multiples of 10 plus 1 with repeat of rows 2–5 consecutively to desired length and either omit last round or work same amount of single crochet on each side edge with 3 single crochet in each corner.

Chain-5 at beginning of row or round counts as first double crochet and chain-2 unless otherwise stated.

Join with slip stitch as indicated unless otherwise stated.

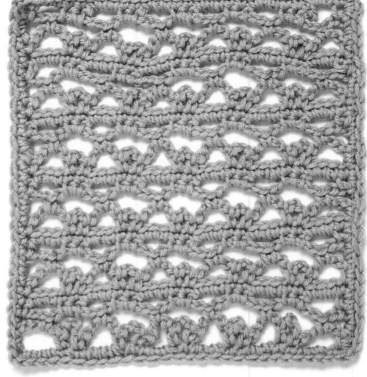

INSTRUCTIONS

Row 1: Ch 31 (see Pattern Notes), sc in 2nd ch from hook, ch 5, sk next 3 chs, [sc in next ch, ch 3, sc in next ch, ch 5, sk next 3 chs] across to last ch, sc in last ch, turn. (5 ch-3 sps, 6 ch-5 sps)

Row 2: Ch 5 (see Pattern Notes), sc in first ch-5 sp, [ch 5, sk next ch-3 sp, sc in next ch-5 sp] across, ch 2, dc in last sc, turn.

Row 3: Ch 1, sc in first st, ch 3, sk next ch sp, 2 sc in next ch sp, [ch 3, 2 sc in next ch sp] 4 times, ch 3, sc in 3rd ch of last ch-5, turn.

Row 4: Ch 1, sc in first st, 3 sc in next ch sp, [sc in each of next 2 sts, 3 sc in next ch sp] across to last st, sc in last st, turn. (30 sc)

Row 5: Ch 1, sc in first st, ch 5, sk next 3 sts, [sc in next st, ch 3, sc in next st, ch 5, sk next 3 sts] across to last st, sc in last st, turn.

Rows 6–23: [Rep rows 2–5 consecutively] 5 times, ending last rep with row 3. At end of last row, **do not turn**.

Rnd 24: Working in ends of rows and in sts with smaller hook, ch 1, evenly sp 25 sc down each edge around with 3 sc in each corner, **join** (see Pattern Notes) in beg sc. Fasten off. ▪

Swatch 69

PATTERN NOTES

Made with 1 color and 2 hook sizes.

For larger Swatch, work chain in multiples of 3 plus 3 with repeat of rows 3 and 4 alternately to desired length and either omit last round or work same amount of single crochet on each side edge with 3 single crochet in each corner.

Chain-3 at beginning of row or round counts as first double crochet unless otherwise stated.

Join with slip stitch as indicated unless otherwise stated.

SPECIAL STITCHES

Cross-stitch (cross-st): Sk next 2 sts, dc in next st, ch 1, working in front of dc just made, dc in first sk st.

Long cross-stitch (long cross-st): Sk next 2 sts, dc in next st, ch 1, working in front of dc just made, yo, insert hook from front to back around post of first dc of next cross-st on row before last, yo, pull up long lp, [yo, pull through 2 lps on hook] twice.

INSTRUCTIONS

Row 1 (WS): Ch 30 *(see Pattern Notes)*, sc in 2nd ch from hook and in each ch across, turn. *(29 sc)*

Row 2: Ch 3 *(see Pattern Notes)*, **cross-st** *(see*

Special Stitches) across, ending with dc in last st, turn. *(2 dc, 9 cross-sts)*

Row 3: Ch 1, sc in each st and in each ch sp across, turn.

Row 4: Ch 3, **long cross-st** *(see Special Stitches)* across to last st, dc in last st, turn.

Rows 5–23: [Rep rows 3 and 4 alternately] 10 times, ending last rep with row 3.

Rnd 24: Working in sts and in ends of rows, with smaller hook, ch 1, evenly sp 25 sc down each edge around with 3 sc in each corner, **join** *(see Pattern Notes)* in beg sc. Fasten off. ▪

Swatch 70

PATTERN NOTES

Made with 1 color and 2 hook sizes.

For larger Swatch, work chain in multiples of 8 plus 7 with repeat of rows 3 and 4 alternately to desired length, ending last repeat with row 3 and either omit last round or work same amount of single crochet on each side edge with 3 single crochet in each corner.

Chain-3 at beginning of row or round counts as first double crochet unless otherwise stated.

Join with slip stitch as indicated unless otherwise stated.

SPECIAL STITCHES

V-stitch (V-st): (Dc, ch 1, dc) as indicated in instructions.

Shell: 5 dc as indicated in instructions.

INSTRUCTIONS

Row 1: Ch 31 (see Pattern Notes), dc in 4th ch form hook (first 3 chs count as first dc) and in each ch across, turn. (29 dc)

Row 2: Ch 3 (see Pattern Notes), sk next st, **V-st** (see Special Stitches) in next st, [sk next 3 sts, **shell** (see Special Stitches) in next st, sk next 3 sts, V-st in next st] across to last 2 sts, sk next st, dc in last st, turn. (2 dc, 3 shells, 4 V-sts)

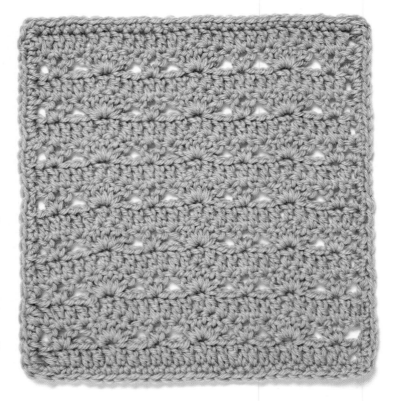

Row 3: Ch 3, dc in each st and in each ch sp across, turn.

Row 4: Ch 3, sk next st, V-st in next st, [sk next 3 sts, shell in next st, sk next 3 sts, V-st in next st] across to last 2 sts, sk next st, dc in last st, turn.

Rows 5–15: [Rep rows 3 and 4 alternately] 6 times, ending last rep with row 3. At end of last row, **do not turn.**

Rnd 16: Working in ends of rows and in sts, with smaller hook, ch 1, evenly sp 25 sc down each edge around with 3 sc in each corner, **join** (see Pattern Notes) in beg sc. Fasten off. ▪

Swatch 71

PATTERN NOTES

Made with 1 color and 2 hook sizes.

For larger Swatch, work chain in multiples of 2 plus 2 with repeat of rows 2 and 3 alternately to desired length, ending last repeat with row 2 and either omit last round or work same amount of single crochet on each side edge with 3 single crochet in each corner.

Join with slip stitch as indicated unless otherwise stated.

INSTRUCTIONS

Row 1: **Ch 30** (*see Pattern Notes*), sc in 2nd ch from hook, [ch 1, sk next ch, sc in next ch] across, turn. (*14 ch sps, 15 sc*)

Row 2: Ch 1, sc in first st, [dc in next ch sp, sc in next st] across, turn.

Row 3: Ch 1, sc in first st, [ch 1, sk next st, sc in next st] across, turn.

Rows 4–28: [Rep rows 2 and 3 alternately] 13 times, ending last rep with row 2.

Rnd 29: Working in sts and in ends of rows, with smaller hook, ch 1, evenly sp 25 sc down each edge around with 3 sc in each corner, **join** (*see Pattern Notes*) in beg sc. Fasten off. ▪

Swatch 72

PATTERN NOTES

Made with 1 color and 2 hook sizes.

For larger Swatch, work chain in multiples of 2 plus 2 with repeat of row 2 to desired length and either omit last round or work same amount of single crochet on each side edge with 3 single crochet in each corner.

Join with slip stitch as indicated unless otherwise stated.

INSTRUCTIONS

Row 1: Ch 26 (*see Pattern Notes*), (sc, ch 2, sc) in 2nd ch from hook, [sk next ch, (sc, ch 2, sc) in next ch] across, turn. (*13 patterns*)

Rows 2–26: Ch 1, (sc, ch 2, sc) in each ch sp across, turn.

Rnd 27: Working in sts and in ends of rows, with smaller hook, ch 1, evenly sp 25 sc down each edge around with 3 sc in each corner, **join** (*see Pattern Notes*) in beg sc. Fasten off. ▪

Swatch 73

PATTERN NOTES
Made with 1 color and 2 hook sizes.

For larger Swatch, work chain in multiples of 3 plus 7 with repeat of rows 2 and 3 alternately to desired length and either omit last round or work same amount of single crochet on each side edge with 3 single crochet in each corner.

Chain-3 at beginning of row or round counts as first double crochet unless otherwise stated.

Join with slip stitch as indicated unless otherwise stated.

SPECIAL STITCHES
Cluster (cl): Holding back last lp of each st on hook, 2 dc as indicated in instructions, yo, pull through all lps on hook.

Shell: (Cl, ch 1, cl) as indicated in instructions.

INSTRUCTIONS
Row 1: Ch 28 *(see Pattern Notes)*, **cl** *(see Special Stitches)* in 4th ch from hook *(first 3 chs count as first dc)*, [sk next 2 chs, **shell** *(see Special Stitches)* in next ch] across to last 3 chs, sk next 2 chs, (cl, dc) in last ch. *(2 dc, 2 cls, 7 shells)*

Row 2: Ch 3 *(see Pattern Notes)*, shell in sp between next cl and next shell, [shell in sp between next 2 shells] across, ending with shell in sp between last shell and last cl, dc in last st, turn. *(2 dc, 8 shells)*

Row 3: Ch 3, cl in same st as beg ch-3, [shell in sp between next 2 shells] across, (cl, dc) in last st, turn.

Rows 4–15: [Rep rows 2 and 3 alternately] 6 times. At end of last row, **do not turn.**

Rnd 16: Working in ends of rows and in sts, with smaller hook, ch 1, evenly sp 25 sc down each edge around with 3 sc in each corner, **join** *(see Pattern Notes)* in beg sc. Fasten off. ▪

Swatch 74

PATTERN NOTES

Made with 1 color and 2 hook sizes.

For larger Swatch, work chain in multiples of 4 plus 7 with repeat of rows 2 and 3 alternately to desired length and either omit last round or work same amount of single crochet on each side edge with 3 single crochet in each corner.

Chain-2 at beginning of row or round counts as first half double crochet unless otherwise stated.

Chain-3 at beginning of row or round counts as first double crochet unless otherwise stated.

Join with slip stitch as indicated unless otherwise stated.

INSTRUCTIONS

Row 1: Ch 31 *(see Pattern Notes)*, dc in 4th ch from hook *(first 3 chs count as first dc)* and in each ch across, turn. *(29 dc)*

Row 2: Ch 2 *(see Pattern Notes)*, **fpdc** *(see Stitch Guide)* around each of next 3 sts, [**bpdc** *(see Stitch Guide)* around next st, fpdc around each of next 3 sts] across, ending with hdc in last st, turn.

Row 3: Ch 3 *(see Pattern Notes)*, [dc in each of next 3 sts, fpdc around next bpdc] across to last 4 sts, dc in each of last 4 sts, turn.

Rows 4–19: [Rep rows 2 and 3 alternately] 8 times. At end of last row, **do not turn**.

Rnd 20: Working in ends of rows and in sts, with smaller hook, ch 1, evenly sp 25 sc down each edge around with 3 sc in each corner, **join** *(see Pattern Notes)* in beg sc. Fasten off. ▪

Swatch 75

PATTERN NOTES
Made with 1 color and 2 hook sizes.

For larger Swatch, work chain in multiples of 12 plus 5 with rep of rows 3–6 consecutively to desired length and either omit last round or work same amount of single crochet on each side edge with 3 single crochet in each corner.

Chain-3 at beginning of row or round counts as first double crochet unless otherwise stated.

Join with slip stitch as indicated unless otherwise stated.

INSTRUCTIONS
Row 1 (WS): **Ch 39** (*see Pattern Notes*), sc in 2nd ch from hook and in each ch across, turn. (*28 sc*)

Row 2: Ch 1, sc in each st across, turn.

Rows 3 & 4: Ch 3 (*see Pattern Notes*), dc in each of next 3 sts, [sk next 2 sts, tr in each of next 2 sts, working behind tr just made, tr in first sk st, tr in 2nd sk st, sk next 2 sts, tr in each of next 2 sts, working in front of tr just made, tr in first sk st, tr in 2nd sk st, dc in each of next 4 sts] across, turn.

Rows 5 & 6: Ch 1, sc in each st across, turn.

Rows 7–18: [Rep rows 3–6 consecutively] 3 times. At end of last row, **do not turn.**

Rnd 19: Working in ends of rows and in sts, with smaller hook, ch 1, evenly sp 25 sc down each edge around with 3 sc in each corner, **join** (*see Pattern Notes*) in beg sc. Fasten off. ▪

Swatch 76

PATTERN NOTES
Made with 1 color and 2 hook sizes.

For larger Swatch, work chain in multiples of 3 plus 4 with repeat of row 3 to desired length and either omit last round or work same amount of single crochet on each side edge with 3 single crochet in each corner.

Chain-3 at beginning of row or round counts as first double crochet unless otherwise stated.

Join with slip stitch as indicated unless otherwise stated.

SPECIAL STITCH
Y-stitch (Y-st): Dc in next st, ch 1, hdc in 2 lower strands of dc *(see illustration)* just made.

**Lower Strands of
Double Crochet**

INSTRUCTIONS
Row 1: Ch 37 *(see Pattern Notes)*, dc in 4th ch from hook *(first 3 chs count as first dc)*, ch 1, hdc in 2 front vertical bars of dc just made *(first Y-st)*, [sk next 2 chs, **Y-st** *(see Special Stitch)* in next ch] across, turn. *(2 dc, 11 Y-sts)*

Row 2: Ch 3 *(see Pattern Notes)*, Y-st in ch sp of each Y-st across, ending with dc in last st, turn.

Rows 3–13: Ch 3, Y-st in ch sp of each Y-st across, ending with dc in last st, turn. At end of last row, **do not turn**.

Rnd 14: Working in ends of rows and in sts, with smaller hook, ch 1, evenly sp 25 sc down each edge around with 3 sc in each corner, **join** *(see Pattern Notes)* in beg sc. Fasten off. ▪

corner st before 1 short end, 2 sc in same st, sc in each st and in each seam around with 3 sc in each corner, **join** (see Pattern Notes) in beg sc. (139 sc across each short edge between center corner sts; 167 sc across each long edge between corner sts)

Rnd 2: Sl st in next st, ch 1, sc in same st as sl st, *sk next 3 sts, (2 dc, ch 1, 2 dc) in next st, [sk next 2 sts, sc in next st, sk next 2 sts, (2 dc, ch 1, 2 dc) in next st] across to 3 sts before center corner st, sk next 3 sts, sc in next corner st, sk next 2 sts, (2 dc, ch 1, 2 dc) in next st, [sk next 2 sts, sc in next st, sk next 2 sts, (2 dc, ch 1, 2 dc) in next st] across to 2 sts before center corner st, sk next 2 sts*, sc in next corner st, rep between * once, join in beg sc.

Rnd 3: Ch 2, (3 dc, ch 1, 3 dc) in next ch sp, ch 2, [sl st in next sc, ch 2, (3 dc, ch 1, 3 dc) in next ch sp, ch 2] around, join in joining sl st of last rnd.

Rnd 4: Ch 3, sk next ch sp, (4 dc, **picot**—see Special Stitch, 4 dc) in next ch sp, ch 3, sk next ch sp, [sl st in next sl st, ch 3, sk next ch sp, (4 dc, picot, 4 dc) in next ch sp, ch 3, sk next ch sp] around, join in joining sl st of last rnd. Fasten off. ▪

SWATCHES 78–81 DESIGNS BY SUSAN LOWMAN

Swatch 78

PATTERN NOTES
Made with 1 color.

For larger Swatch, work in multiples of 8 chains plus 9 with repeat of rows 3–9 consecutively to desired length, ending with row 3 and either omit Edging or work same amount of single crochet on each side edge with 3 single crochet in each corner.

Join with slip stitch as indicated unless otherwise stated.

SPECIAL STITCH
Berry stitch (berry st): Insert hook as indicated in instructions, yo, pull up lp, [yo, pull through 1 lp on hook] 3 times, yo, pull through all lps on hook.

INSTRUCTIONS
Row 1 (WS): Beg at bottom of Swatch, **ch 26** (see *Pattern Notes*), sc in 2nd ch from hook and in each ch across, turn (*25 sc*)

Row 2: Ch 1, sc in each of first 4 sc, [**berry st** (see *Special Stitch*) in next sc, sc in each of next 7 sc] across to last 5 sts, berry st in next sc, sc in each of last 4 sc, turn.

Row 3: Ch 1, sc in each st across, turn.

Row 4: Ch 1, sc in each of first 3 sc, *berry st in next sc, sc in next sc, berry st in next sc**, sc in each of next 5 sc, rep from * across, ending last rep at **, sc in each of last 3 sc, turn.

Row 5: Rep row 3.

Row 6: Ch 1, sc in each of first 2 sc, *[berry st in next sc, sc in next sc] twice, berry st in next sc**, sc in each of next 3 sc, rep from * across, ending last rep at **, sc in each of last 2 sc, turn.

Rows 7 & 8: Rep rows 3 and 4.

Row 9: Rep row 3.

Row 10: Ch 1, sc in each of next 4 sc, [berry st in next sc, sc in each of next 3 sc] across to last 5 sts, berry st in next sc, sc in each of next 4 sc, turn.

Row 11: Rep row 3.

Row 12: Ch 1, sc in each of first 7 sc, *[berry st in next sc, sc in next sc, berry st in next sc*, sc in each of next 5 sc, rep between * once] across to last 7 sts, sc in each of last 7 sc, turn.

Row 13: Rep row 3.

Row 14: Ch 1, sc in each of first 6 sc, ◊*[berry st in next sc, sc in next sc] twice, berry st in next sc*, sc in each of next 3 sc, rep between * once, rep from ◊ across to last 6 sts, sc in each of last 6 sc, turn.

Row 15: Rep row 3.

Row 16: Rep row 12.

Row 17: Rep row 3.

Row 18: Rep row 10.

Rows 19–25: Rep rows 3–9.

Rows 26 & 27: Rep rows 2 and 3. At the end of row 27, **do not fasten off.**

EDGING

Ch 1, 2 sc in first sc, sc in each of next 23 sc, 3 sc in last sc, working along left edge, [sc in edge of each of next 5 rows, **sc dec** (*see Stitch Guide*) in edge of next 2 rows] 3 times, sc in edge of last 5 rows, working in opposite side of row 1, 3 sc in first ch, sc in each of next 23 chs, 3 sc in last ch, working along right edge, sc in each of next 5 rows, [sc dec in edge of next 2 rows, sc in edge of each of next 5 rows] 3 times, sc in same st as first 2-sc, **join** (*see Pattern Notes*) in first sc. Fasten off. ▪

Swatch 79

PATTERN NOTES

Made with 1 color.

For larger Swatch, work chains in multiples of 8 plus 12 with repeat of rows 3–13 consecutively to desired length, then work last 2 rows and either omit Edging or work same amount of single crochet on each side edge with 3 single crochet in each corner.

Join with slip stitch as indicated unless otherwise stated.

SPECIAL STITCHES

Cluster (cl): Holding back last lp of each st on hook, 4 dc as indicated in instructions, yo, pull through all lps on hook.

Front post double crochet decrease (fpdc dec): *Yo, insert hook front to back to front around top of next cl, yo, draw up lp, yo, draw through 2 lps on hook*, yo, insert hook front to back to front around post of next fpdc, yo, draw up lp, yo, draw through 2 lps on hook, rep from * to *, yo, draw through all 4 lps on hook. Sk st behind fpdc dec on this row.

INSTRUCTIONS

Row 1 (WS): Starting at top, **ch 26** (*see Pattern Notes*), sc in 2nd ch from hook and in each ch across, turn. (*25 sc*)

Row 2: Ch 1, sc in each of first 8 sc, **cl** (*see Special Stitches*) in next sc, [sc in each of next 7 sc, cl in next sc] across to last 8 sc, sc in each of last 8 sc, turn.

Row 3: Ch 1, sc in each st across, turn.

Row 4: Ch 1, sc in each of first 6 sc, [*cl in next sc, sc in next sc, **fpdc** *(see Stitch Guide)* around next cl, sc in next sc, cl in next sc*, sc in each of next 3 sc, rep between * once] across to last 6 sts, sc in each of last 6 sc, turn.

Row 5: Rep row 3.

Row 6: Ch 1, sc in each of first 8 sc, **fpdc dec** *(see Special Stitches)*, [sc in each of next 7 sc, fpdc dec] across to last 8 sc, sc in each of last 8 sc, turn.

Row 7: Rep row 3.

Row 8: Ch 1, sc in each of first 4 sc, [cl in next sc, sc in each of next 3 sc, fpdc around next fpdc dec, sc in next 3 sc] across to last 5 sc, cl in next sc, sc in each of last 4 sc, turn.

Row 9: Rep row 3.

Row 10: Ch 1, sc in each of next 2 sc, *cl in next sc, sc in next sc, fpdc around next cl, sc in next sc, cl in next sc**, sc in each of next 3 sc, rep from * across, ending last rep at **, sc in each of last 2 sc, turn.

Row 11: Rep row 3.

Row 12: Ch 1, sc in each of first 4 sc, *fpdc dec**, sc in each of next 7 sc, rep from * across, ending last rep at **, sc in each of last 4 sc, turn.

Row 13: Rep row 3.

Row 14: Ch 1, sc in each of first 4 sc, *fpdc around next fpdc dec**, sc in each of next 3 sc, cl in next sc, sc in each of next 3 sc, rep from * across, ending last rep at **, sc in each of last 4 sc, turn.

Rows 15–25: Rep rows 3–13.

Row 26: Ch 1, sc in each of first 4 sc, [fpdc around next fpdc dec, sc in each of next 7 sc] across, ending with fpdc around next fpdc dec, sc in each of last 4 sc, turn.

Row 27: Rep row 3. Do not fasten off.

EDGING

Ch 1, 2 sc in first sc, sc in each of next 23 sc, 3 sc in last sc, working along left edge, [sc in edge of each of next 5 rows, **sc dec** *(see Stitch Guide)* in edge of next 2 rows] 3 times, sc in edge of last 5 rows, working in opposite side of row 1, 3 sc in first ch, sc in each of next 23 chs, 3 sc in last ch, working along right edge, sc in each of next 5 rows, [sc dec in edge of next 2 rows, sc in edge of each of next 5 rows] 3 times, sc in same st as first 2 sc, **join** *(see Pattern Notes)* in first sc. Fasten off. ▪

Swatch 80

PATTERN NOTES
Made with 1 color.

For larger Swatch, work chains in multiples of 23 plus 3 with repeat of rows 3–6 consecutively to desired length, ending with row 4, then work last row and either omit Edging or work same amount of single crochet on each side edge with 3 single crochet in each corner.

Chain-3 at beginning of row or round counts as first double crochet unless otherwise stated.

Join with slip stitch as indicated unless otherwise stated.

SPECIAL STITCHES
Front post extended double crochet (fp ext dc): Yo, insert hook front to back to front around post of indicated st in instructions, yo, pull up lp, yo, pull through 1 lp on hook, [yo, pull through 2 lps on hook] twice.

Back post extended double crochet (bp ext dc): Yo, insert hook back to front to back around post of indicated st in instructions, yo, pull up lp, yo, pull through 1 lp on hook, [yo, pull through 2 lps on hook] twice.

Popcorn (pc): 5 dc in indicated st in instructions, drop lp from hook, insert hook in first dc of dc group, pull dropped lp through.

INSTRUCTIONS
Row 1 (WS): Starting at bottom, **ch 26** (see Pattern Notes), sc in 2nd ch from hook and in each ch across, turn. (25 sc)

Row 2: Ch 3 (see Pattern Notes), dc in each sc across, turn.

Row 3: Ch 3, [*fp ext dc (see Special Stitches) around each of next 2 sts, dc in next st, ch 1, sk next st, pc (see Special Stitches) in next st, ch 1, sk next st, dc in next st, fp ext dc around each of next 2 sts*, dc in each of next 5 sts, rep between * once] across, dc in 3rd ch of beg ch-3, turn.

Row 4: Ch 3, [*bp ext dc (see Special Stitches) around each of next 2 fp ext dc, dc in next dc, dc in next ch-1 sp, dc in next pc, dc in next ch-1 sp, dc in next dc, bp ext dc around each of next 2 fp ext dc*, dc in each of next 5 sts, rep between * once] across, dc in 3rd ch of beg ch-3, turn.

Row 5: Ch 3, [*fp ext dc around each of next 2 bp ext dc, dc in each of next 5 dc, fp ext dc around each of next 2 bp ext dc*, dc in next dc, ch 1, sk next dc, pc in next dc, ch 1, sk next dc, dc in next dc, rep between * once] across, dc in 3rd ch of beg ch-3, turn.

Row 6: Ch 3, [*bp ext dc around each of next 2 fp ext dc, dc in each of next 5 dc, bp ext dc around each of next 2 bp ext dc*, dc in next dc, dc in next ch-1 sp, dc in next pc, dc in next ch-1 sp, dc in next dc, rep between * once, dc in 3rd ch of beg ch-3, turn.

Rows 7–10: Rep rows 3–6.

Rows 11 & 12: Rep rows 3 and 4.

Row 13: Ch 1, sc in each st across, **Do not fasten off.**

EDGING
Ch 1, working along left edge, [sc in top of next dc, sc around post of same dc] 11 times, sc in edge of row 1, working across opposite side of foundation ch, 3 sc in first ch, sc in each of next 23 chs, 3 sc in last ch, working along right edge, sc in edge of row 1, [sc around post of next dc, sc in top of same dc] 11 times, working along top edge, 3 sc in first st, sc in each of next 23 sts, 3 sc in last st, join in first sc. Fasten off. ▪

Swatch 81

PATTERN NOTES
Made with 1 color.

For larger Swatch, work chains in multiples of 9 plus 7 with repeat of rows 3 and 4 alternately to desired length, ending with row 3, then work last row and either omit Edging or work same amount of single crochet on each side edge with 3 single crochet in each corner.

Join with slip stitch as indicated unless otherwise stated.

SPECIAL STITCH
Braid: Sk next st, fptr around each of next 2 sts 1 row below, working in front of last 2 sts, fptr around sk st 1 row below.

INSTRUCTIONS
Row 1 (WS): Starting at bottom, **ch 26** (see *Pattern Notes*), sc in 2nd ch from hook and in each ch across, turn.

Row 2: Ch 3, dc in each sc across, turn.

Row 3: Ch 1, sc in each st across, turn.

Row 4: Ch 3, dc in next st, *fptr (see *Stitch Guide*) around next dc 1 row below next st, **braid** (see *Special Stitch*) in next 3 sts 1 row below, fptr around next dc 1 row below next st**, dc in each of next 3 sts, rep from * across, ending last rep at **, dc in each of last 2 sts, turn.

Rows 5–20: [Rep rows 3 and 4 alternately] 8 times.

Row 21: Rep row 3. **Do not fasten off.**

EDGING
Ch 1, 2 sc in first sc, sc in each of next 23 sc, 3 sc in last sc, working along left edge, *[sc around post of next dc, sc in edge of next sc] twice, sc in top of next dc, sc around post of same dc, sc in edge of next sc, rep from * twice, sc around post of next dc, sc in edge of next sc, working on opposite side of starting ch on row 1, 3 sc in first ch, sc in each of next 23 chs, 3 sc in last ch, working along right edge, sc in edge of next sc, sc around post of next dc, **sc in edge of next sc, sc around post of next dc, sc in top of same dc, sc in edge of next sc, sc around post of next dc] twice, rep from ** twice, sc in same st as first 2-sc, join in first sc. Fasten off. ▪

Patchwork Squares
Afghan

DESIGN BY SUSAN LOWMAN

SKILL LEVEL

INTERMEDIATE

FINISHED SIZE
50½ x 66½ inches

MATERIALS
- Bernat Super Value medium (worsted) weight yarn (7 oz/382 yds/197g per ball): **MEDIUM**
  - 2 balls #53522 redwood heather (A)
  - 1 ball each #53223 grass (G), #53332 grape (H)
- Bernat Berella 4 medium (worsted) weight yarn (3½ oz/195 yds/100g per ball):
  - 3 balls each #8886 light tapestry gold (B), #1242 deep forest green (C), #1012 true taupe (D) and #1514 topaz (F)
  - 2 balls #8927 burgundy (E)
- Size I/9/5.5mm crochet hook or size needed to obtain gauge
- Tapestry needle

GAUGE
Swatch with Edging = 8 inches; 14 sc = 4 inches; 15 sc rows = 4 inches

PATTERN NOTE
Join with slip stitch as indicated unless otherwise stated.

SPECIAL STITCH
Back loop single crochet decrease (back lp sc dec): Working in back lps, insert hook in center sc at last corner of current square, yo, draw up lp, insert hook in center sc at first corner of next square, yo, draw up lp, yo, draw through all 3 lps on hook.

Patchwork Squares Afghan
Placement Diagram

SQUARE TYPE
1—Swatch 78
2—Swatch 79
3—Swatch 80
4—Swatch 81

COLOR KEY
■ Redwood heather
▨ Light tapestry gold
■ Deep forest green
▨ True taupe
■ Burgundy
□ Topaz
▨ Grass
■ Grape

INSTRUCTIONS
AFGHAN
Using Swatches 78–81, make 2 Swatches with each color A–D and 1 Swatch with each color E–H to equal 12 Swatches, 3 of each Swatch design.

ASSEMBLY
Referring to Placement Diagram on page 91, join Swatches tog in 8 rows of 6 Swatches each.

To join, hold 2 Swatches with RS tog, matching sts, **join** (see Pattern Note) F in **back lp** (see Stitch Guide) of center sc in corner of both Swatches, working through both thicknesses **at same time** and in back lps, sl st in each sc across to next corner, hold next 2 Swatches tog and join in same manner.

Join rem Swatches in same manner, joining Swatches in rows.

Join rows tog in same manner using care that all 4-corner junctions are secure.

BORDER
Rnd 1: With RS facing and working in back lp of each st around, join F with sc in center sc in any corner, sc in same sc as joining, sc in each sc around, working 3 sc in center sc of each corner and **back lp sc dec** (see Special Stitch) in center sc at joining of Square; sc in same sc as joining, join in first sc.

Rnd 2: Ch 1, 2 sc in same sc as joining, sc in back lp of next sc, *sc in next sc, sc in back lp of next sc, rep from * across to next corner**, 3 sc in center sc in next corner, sc in back lp of next sc, rep from * around, ending last rep at **, sc in same sc as first 2 sc, join in first sc.

Rnd 3: Ch 1, 2 sc in same sc as joining, sc in back lp of next sc, berry st in next sc, *sc in back lp of next sc, sc in next sc, sc in back lp of next sc, berry st in next sc, rep from * across to next corner, sc in back lp of next sc**, 3 sc in center sc of 3-sc in corner, sc in back lp of next sc, berry st in next sc, rep from * around, ending last rep at **, sc in same sc as first 2-sc, join in first sc.

Rnd 4: Ch 1, (sc, ch 5, sc) in same sc as joining, ch 3, sc in back lp of next sc, *[sc in next sc, sc in back lp of next sc, sc in next sc, (sc, ch 3, sc) in back lp of next sc] across to last 4 sts before next corner, [sc in next sc, sc in back lp of next sc] twice, ch 3**, (sc, ch 5, sc) in next sc, ch 3, sc in back lp of next sc, rep from * around, ending last rep at **, join in first sc. Fasten off. ▪

EDGINGS
DESIGNS BY BELINDA "BENDY" CARTER

Edging 82

PATTERN NOTES
Made with 2 colors.

Join with slip stitch as indicated unless otherwise stated.

INSTRUCTIONS
Foundation rnd: With first color, working in multiples of 3 with ch-2 at each corner, evenly sp sc around, **join** (see Pattern Notes) in beg sc. Fasten off first color.

Rnd 2: Join 2nd color with sc in any corner ch-2 sp, ch 2, sc around posts of last 2 sts **at same time**, ch 3, sl st in 3rd ch from hook, 2 sc in same ch sp as beg sc, ch 2, sc around post of last 2 sts **at same time**, *sk next st, [sc dec (see Stitch Guide) in next 2 sts, sc around post of last 2 sc **at same time**] across to next corner ch sp**, (2 sc, ch 2, sc around posts of last 2 sts **at same time**, ch 3, sl st in 3rd ch from hook, 2 sc, ch 2, sc around post of last 2 sts **at same time**) in next corner ch sp, rep from * around, ending last rep at **, join in beg sc. Fasten off. ▪

Edging 83

PATTERN NOTES
Made with 2 colors.

Join with slip stitch as indicated unless otherwise stated.

INSTRUCTIONS
Foundation rnd (RS): With first color, working in multiples of 7, evenly sp sc around with ch-2 at each corner, **join** (see Pattern Notes) in beg sc. Fasten off first color.

Rnd 2: With RS facing, join 2nd color with sc in any corner ch sp, (dc, sl st around post of last dc made, ch 1, dc, sl st around post of last dc made) in same ch sp, *sl st in next st, [sc in next st, hdc in next st, **dc dec** (see Stitch Guide) in next 2 sts, tr in same st as 2nd st of last dc dec, sl st twice in side of last tr made, sl st in next st] across to next corner ch sp**, (sc, dc, sl st around post of last dc made, sl st, ch 1, dc, sl st around post of last dc made) in next corner, rep from * around, ending last rep at **, join in beg sc. Fasten off. ▪

Edging 84

PATTERN NOTES

Made with 2 colors.

Join with slip stitch as indicated unless otherwise stated.

INSTRUCTIONS

Foundation rnd (RS): With first color, working in multiples of any number, evenly sp sc around with ch-2 at each corner, **join** (see Pattern Notes) in beg sc. Fasten off first color.

Rnd 2: With RS facing, join 2nd color with sc in any corner ch sp, ch 1, sc in same ch sp, sc in each st around with (sc, ch 1, sc) in each corner ch sp, join in beg sc.

Rnd 3: Ch 1, working from left to right, **reverse sc** (see Stitch Guide) in each st and in each ch around, join in beg reverse sc. Fasten off. ▪

Edging 85

PATTERN NOTES

Made with 2 colors.

Join with slip stitch as indicated unless otherwise stated.

SPECIAL STITCH

Pointed fringe: Ch 5, sl st in back bar (see illustration) of 2nd ch from hook, sc in back bar of next ch, dc in back bar of next ch, sc in back bar of last ch.

Back Bar of Chain

INSTRUCTIONS

Foundation rnd (RS): With first color, working in multiples of 2 plus 1 between each corner ch sp, evenly sp sc around with ch-2 at each corner, **join** (see Pattern Notes) in beg sc. Fasten off first color.

Rnd 2: With RS facing, join 2nd color in any corner ch sp, (**pointed fringe**—see Special Stitch, sl st) twice in same corner ch sp, *sk next st, [sl st in next st, pointed fringe, sl st in same st as last sl st, sk next st] across to next corner ch sp**, (sl st, {pointed fringe, sl st} twice) in next corner ch sp, rep from * around, ending last rep at **, join in beg sl st. Fasten off. ▪

Edging 86

PATTERN NOTES
Made with 2 colors.

Join with slip stitch as indicated unless otherwise stated.

INSTRUCTIONS
Foundation rnd (RS): With first color, working in multiples of 2 plus 1 between each corner ch sp, evenly sp sc around with ch-2 at each corner, **join** (*see Pattern Notes*) in beg sc. Fasten off first color.

Rnd 2: With RS facing, join 2nd color with sc in any corner ch sp, ch 1, sc in same ch sp, sc in each st around with (sc, ch 1, sc) in each corner ch sp, join in beg sc.

Rnd 3: Sl st in next ch sp, ch 1, (hdc, ch 2, hdc) in same ch sp, *sl st in next st, [hdc in next st, sl st in next st] across to next corner ch sp**, (hdc, ch 2, hdc) in next corner ch sp, rep from * around, ending last rep at **, join in beg hdc. Fasten off. ▪

Edging 87

PATTERN NOTES
Made with 2 colors.

Join with slip stitch as indicated unless otherwise stated.

INSTRUCTIONS
Foundation rnd (RS): With first color, working in multiples of 2 plus 1 between each corner ch sp, evenly sp sc around with ch-2 at each corner, **join** (*see Pattern Notes*) in beg sc. Fasten off first color.

Rnd 2: With RS facing, join 2nd color in any corner ch sp, (ch 3, sl st) 3 times in same ch sp, *[sk next st, (sl st, ch 3, sl st) in next st] across to last st before next corner ch sp, sk next st**, (sl st, {ch 3, sl st} 3 times) in next corner ch sp, rep from * around, ending last rep at **, join in beg sl st. Fasten off. ▪

Edging 88

PATTERN NOTES
Made with 2 colors.

Join with slip stitch as indicated unless otherwise stated.

SPECIAL STITCH
Cluster (cl): Ch 2, yo, insert hook in last worked st, yo, pull lp through, yo, pull through 2 lps on hook, yo, insert hook in same st, yo, pull lp through, yo, pull through 2 lps on hook, insert hook in next st, yo, pull through st and through all lps on hook.

INSTRUCTIONS
Foundation rnd (RS): With first color, working in multiples of any number, evenly sp sc around with ch-2 at each corner, **join** (*see Pattern Notes*) in beg sc. Fasten off first color.

Rnd 2: With RS facing, join 2nd color in any corner ch sp, *ch 2, [yo, insert hook in same ch sp, yo, pull lp through, yo, pull through 2 lps on hook] twice, insert hook in next st, yo, pull through st and through 3 lps on hook, **cl** (*see Special Stitch*) across to next corner ch sp, ch 2, yo, insert hook in last worked st, yo, pull lp through, yo, pull through 2 lps on hook, yo, insert hook in same st, yo, pull lp through, yo, pull through 2 lps on hook, insert hook in next corner ch sp, yo, pull through sp and through 3 lps on hook, rep from * around, working last st of last cl in same ch sp as joining sl st. Fasten off. ▪

Edging 89

PATTERN NOTES
Made with 2 colors.

Join with slip stitch as indicated unless otherwise stated.

Chain-3 at beginning of row or round counts as first double crochet unless otherwise stated.

SPECIAL STITCHES
Cross-stitch (cross-st): Sk next 2 sts, dtr in next st, working behind last dtr, dc in 2nd sk st, working in front of last dtr, dtr in first sk st.

Corner cross-stitch (corner cross-st): Dtr in corner ch sp, working behind last dtr, dc in same ch sp on right-hand side of last dtr, working in front of last dtr and dc, dtr in same ch sp on right-hand side of last dc.

INSTRUCTIONS
Foundation rnd (RS): With first color, working in multiples of 5, evenly sp sc around with ch-2 at each corner, **join** (*see Pattern Notes*) in beg sc. Fasten off first color.

Rnd 2: With RS facing, join 2nd color in any corner ch sp, **ch 3** (*see Pattern Notes*), (**corner cross-st**—*see Special Stitches*, dc) in same ch sp as beg ch-3, *sk next st, [dc in next st, **cross-st**—*see Special Stitches*, dc in next st] across to next corner ch sp**, (dc, corner cross-st, dc) in next corner ch sp, rep from * around, ending last rep at **, join in 3rd ch of beg ch-3. Fasten off. ▪

Edging 90

PATTERN NOTES
Made with 2 colors.

Join with slip stitch as indicated unless otherwise stated.

INSTRUCTIONS
Foundation rnd (RS): With first color, working in multiples of 4 plus 1 between corner ch sps, evenly sp sc around with ch-2 at each corner, **join** *(see Pattern Notes)* in beg sc. Fasten off first color.

Rnd 2: With RS facing, join 2nd color in any corner ch sp, (sc, ch 1, sc around post of last sc made, sc) in same ch sp, *ch 1, sk next st, [sc in each of 2 sts, ch 1, sc around post of last sc made, sc in next st, ch 1, sk next st] across to next corner ch sp**, (2 sc, ch 1, sc around post of last sc made, sc) in next ch sp, rep from * around, ending last rep at **, join in beg sc. Fasten off. ▪

Edging 91

PATTERN NOTES
Made with 2 colors.

Join with slip stitch as indicated unless otherwise stated.

SPECIAL STITCH
Triple loop stitch (tr lp st): Sl st as indicated in instructions, ch 1, sc in same place as beg sl st, [ch 3, sc around post of last sc made] 3 times, sc around post of first sc.

INSTRUCTIONS
Foundation rnd (RS): With first color, working in multiples of 5 plus 6 between corner ch sps, evenly sp sc around with ch-2 at each corner, **join** *(see Pattern Notes)* in beg sc. Fasten off first color.

Rnd 2: With RS facing, join 2nd color in any corner ch sp, sc in same ch sp as beg sl st, [ch 3, sc around post of last sc made] 3 times, sc around post of first sc, *sl st in next st, hdc in next st, sl st in next st, **tr lp st** *(see Special Stitch)* in next st, [sl st in next st, hdc in each of next 2 sts, sl st in next st, tr lp st in next st] across to 2 sts before next corner ch sp, sl st in next st, hdc in next st**, tr lp st in next corner ch sp, rep from * around, ending last rep at **, join in beg sl st. Fasten off. ▪

Edging 92

PATTERN NOTES
Made with 2 colors.

Join with slip stitch as indicated unless otherwise stated.

INSTRUCTIONS
Foundation rnd (RS): With first color, working in multiples of 2 plus 1 between corner ch sps, evenly sp sc around with ch-2 at each corner, **join** (*see Pattern Notes*) in beg sc. Fasten off first color.

Rnd 2: With RS facing, join 2nd color with sc in any corner ch sp, ch 2, sc in same ch sp as joining sc, sc in each st around with (sc, ch 2, sc) in each corner ch sp, join in beg sc.

Rnd 3: (Sl st, ch 1, sc, ch 2, sc) in first ch sp, *fpsc (*see Stitch Guide*) around next st, [bpsc (*see Stitch Guide*) around next st, fpsc around next st] across to next corner ch sp**, (sc, ch 2, sc) in next ch sp, rep from * around, ending last rep at **, join in beg sc. Fasten off. ▪

Edging 93

PATTERN NOTES
Made with 2 colors.

Join with slip stitch as indicated unless otherwise stated.

Chain-4 at beginning of row or round counts as first half double crochet and chain-2 unless otherwise stated.

SPECIAL STITCH
Cross-stitch (cross-st): Sk next st, dc in next st, working over last dc made, sc in st just sk.

INSTRUCTIONS
Foundation rnd (RS): With first color, working in multiples of 2 plus 3 between corner ch sps, evenly sp sc around with ch-2 at each corner, **join** (*see Pattern Notes*) in beg sc. Fasten off first color.

Rnd 2: With RS facing, join 2nd color in any corner ch sp, **ch 4** (*see Pattern Notes*), hdc in same ch sp as beg ch-4, *sk next 2 sts, dc in next st, working over last dc made, sc in 2nd sk st, **cross-st** (*see Special Stitch*) across to next corner ch sp**, (hdc, ch 2, hdc) in next ch sp, rep from * around, ending last rep at **, join in 2nd ch of beg ch-2. Fasten off. ▪

Edging 94

PATTERN NOTES
Made with 2 colors.

Join with slip stitch as indicated unless otherwise stated.

SPECIAL STITCH
Spring stitch (spring st): Yo 4 times, insert hook as indicated in instructions, yo, pull lp through, yo, pull through all lps on hook.

INSTRUCTIONS
Foundation rnd (RS): With first color, working in multiples of 2 plus 1 between corner ch sps,

evenly sp sc around with ch-2 at each corner, **join** (*see Pattern Notes*) in beg sc. Fasten off first color.

Rnd 2: With RS facing, join 2nd color in any corner ch sp, ch 1, (**spring st**—*see Special Stitch*, ch 2, spring st) in same ch sp as joining sl st, *sl st in next st, [spring st in next st, sl st in next st] across to next corner ch sp**, (spring st, ch 2, spring st) in next ch sp, rep from * around, ending last rep at **, join in beg spring st. Fasten off. ▪

Edging 95

PATTERN NOTES
Made with 2 colors.

Join with slip stitch as indicated unless otherwise stated.

SPECIAL STITCH
Fringe stitch (fringe st): Pull up lp 3 inches tall, turn hook clockwise 7 times, sl st in top of last st made.

INSTRUCTIONS
Foundation rnd (RS): With first color, working in multiples of number, evenly sp sc around

with ch-2 at each corner, **join** (*see Pattern Notes*) in beg sc. Fasten off first color.

Rnd 2: With RS facing, join 2nd color in any corner ch sp, **fringe st** (*see Special Stitch*), (sc, fringe st) twice in same ch sp as joining sl st, *[sc in next st, fringe st] across to next corner ch sp**, (sc, fringe st) 3 times in next corner ch sp, rep from * around, ending last rep at **, join in beg sc. Fasten off. ▪

Edging 96

PATTERN NOTES
Made with 2 colors.

Join with slip stitch as indicated unless otherwise stated.

SPECIAL STITCH
Spike: Ch 3, sl st in **back bar** (see illustration) of 2nd ch from hook, sl st in back bar of last ch.

Back Bar of Chain

INSTRUCTIONS
Foundation rnd (RS): With first color, working in multiples of 2 plus 1 between corner ch sps, evenly sp sc around with ch-2 at each corner, **join** (see Pattern Notes) in beg sc. Fasten off first color.

Rnd 2: With RS facing, join 2nd color in any corner ch sp, (**spike**—see Special Stitch, sl st) 3 times in same ch sp as joining sl st, *[sl st in each of next 2 sts, spike] across to last st before next corner ch sp, sl st in next st**, (sl st, {spike, sl st} 3 times) in next corner ch sp, rep from * around, ending last rep at **, join in beg sl st. Fasten off. ∎

Edging 97

PATTERN NOTES
Made with 2 colors.

Join with slip stitch as indicated unless otherwise stated.

INSTRUCTIONS
Foundation rnd (RS): With first color, working in multiples of 2 plus 1 between corner ch sps, evenly sp sc around with ch-2 at each corner, **join** (see Pattern Notes) in beg sc. Fasten off first color.

Rnd 2: With RS facing, join 2nd color with sc in any corner ch sp, ch 1, sc in same ch sp as beg sc, sc in each st around with (sc, ch 1, sc) in each corner ch sp, join in beg sc.

Rnd 3: Sl st in next ch sp, *ch 3, sl st in **front lp** (see Stitch Guide) of next st, [ch 3, sl st in **back lp** (see Stitch Guide) of next st, ch 3, sl st in front lp of next st] across to next corner ch sp**, (ch 3, sl st) twice in next ch sp, rep from * around, ending last rep at **, ch 3, sl st in beg ch sp, ch 3, join in beg sl st. Fasten off. ∎

Edging 98

PATTERN NOTES
Made with 2 colors.

Join with slip stitch as indicated unless otherwise stated.

INSTRUCTIONS
Foundation rnd (RS): With first color, working in multiples of 2 plus 1 between corner ch sps, evenly sp sc around with ch-2 at each corner, **join** (see Pattern Notes) in beg sc. Fasten off first color.

Rnd 2: With RS facing, join 2nd color with sc in any corner ch sp, ch 4, sc in **back lp** (see Stitch Guide) of 2nd ch from hook, sc in back lps of each of next 2 chs, sl st in same ch sp, *sl st in next st on Edging, [**turn**, sk next 2 sl sts, sc in back lp of each of next 3 sts, **turn**, ch 1, sc in

back lp of each of next 3 sts, sl st in each of next 2 sts on Edging] across to next corner ch sp, **turn**, sk next 2 sl sts, sc in back lp of each of next 3 sts, **turn**, ch 1, sc in back lp of each of next 3 sts**, [sl st in corner ch sp, **turn**, sk next sl st, sc in back lp of each of next 3 sts, **turn**, sc in back lp of each of next 3 sts] twice, sl st in same sp, rep from * around, ending last rep at **, sl st in same ch sp as beg sl st, **turn**, sk next sl st, sc in back lp of each of next 3 sts. Fasten off.

Sew opposite side of ch-4 to last 3 sts. ▪

Edging 99

PATTERN NOTES
Made with 2 colors.

Join with slip stitch as indicated unless otherwise stated.

SPECIAL STITCH
Picot: Ch 3, sl st in **back bar** (see illustration) of 2nd ch from hook, ch 1.

Back Bar of Chain

INSTRUCTIONS
Foundation rnd (RS): With first color, working in multiples of 2 plus 1 between corner ch sps, evenly sp sc around with ch-2 at each corner,

join (see Pattern Notes) in beg sc. Fasten off first color.

Rnd 2: With RS facing, join 2nd color with sc in any corner ch sp, ch 2, sc in same ch sp as beg sc, sc in each st around with (sc, ch 2, sc) in each corner ch sp, join in beg sc.

Rnd 3: Sl st in first ch sp, ch 1, (sc, **picot**—see Special Stitch) 3 times in same ch sp, *sk next st, [sc in next st, picot, sk next st] across to next corner ch sp**, (sc, picot) 3 times in next ch sp, rep from * around, ending last rep at **, join in beg sc. Fasten off. ▪

Edging 100

PATTERN NOTES

Made with 2 colors.

Join with slip stitch as indicated unless otherwise stated.

SPECIAL STITCH

Puff stitch (puff st): Yo, insert hook in st, yo, pull up long lp, yo, insert hook in same st, yo, pull up long lp, yo, pull through all lps on hook, ch 2, sl st in **back bar** (*see illustration*) of 2nd ch from hook.

Back Bar of Chain

INSTRUCTIONS

Foundation rnd (RS): With first color, working in multiples of 2 plus 1 between corner ch sps, evenly sp sc around with ch-2 at each corner, **join** (*see Pattern Notes*) in beg sc. Fasten off first color.

Rnd 2: With RS facing, join 2nd color in any corner ch sp, ch 2, 2 **puff sts** (*see Special Stitch*) in same ch sp as beg sl st, *puff st in next st, [sk next st, puff st in next st] across to next corner ch sp**, 2 puff sts in next ch sp, rep from * around, ending last rep at **, join in 2nd ch of beg ch-2. Fasten off. ▪

Edging 101

PATTERN NOTES

Made with 2 colors.

Join with slip stitch as indicated unless otherwise stated.

SPECIAL STITCH

Curve stitch (curve st): Sc as indicated in instructions, [ch 1, sc in side of last st made] 3 times.

INSTRUCTIONS

Foundation rnd (RS): With first color, working in multiples of 4 plus 1 between corner ch sps, evenly sp sc around with ch-2 at each corner, **join** (*see Pattern Notes*) in beg sc. Fasten off first color.

Rnd 2: With RS facing, join 2nd color in any corner ch sp, [ch 1, sc in side of last sc] 3 times, counting corner ch sps as 1 st, sk next 3 sts, sc in next st, *drop lp from hook, working on front side of work, insert hook in 2nd sk st, pull dropped lp through, ch 1, **curve st** (*see Special Stitch*) in same st, sk next 3 sts, sc in next st, rep from * around, ending last st in same sp as first st behind first curve st. Fasten off. ▪

BASICS

LESSON 1:
Getting Started

To crochet, you need only a crochet hook, some yarn and a tapestry needle.

YARN

Yarn comes in many sizes, from fine crochet cotton used for doilies, to wonderful bulky mohairs used for afghans and sweaters. The most commonly used yarn is medium (or worsted) weight. It is readily available in a wide variety of beautiful colors. This is the weight we will use in our lessons.

Always read yarn labels carefully. The label will tell you how many ounces, grams, meters and/or yards are in the skein or ball of yarn. Read the label to find out the fiber content of the yarn, its washability, and sometimes, how to pull the yarn from the skein. Also, there is usually a dye-lot number on the label. This number assures you that the color of each skein with this number is the same. Yarn of the same color name may vary in shade somewhat from dye lot to dye lot, creating variations in color when a project is completed. Therefore, when purchasing yarn for a project, it is important to match the dye-lot numbers on the skeins. You'll need a blunt-pointed sewing needle with an eye big enough to carry the yarn for weaving in yarn ends and sewing seams. This is a size 16 steel tapestry needle. You can buy big plastic needles called yarn needles, but they are not as good as the steel.

HOOKS

Crochet hooks come in many sizes, from very fine steel hooks, used to make intricate doilies and lace, to very large ones of plastic or wood, used to make bulky sweaters or rugs.

The hooks you will use most often are made of aluminum, are about 6 inches long and are sized alphabetically by letter from B (*smallest*) to K. For our lessons, you'll need a size H hook, which is considered a medium-sized hook.

The aluminum crochet hook looks like this:

In Fig. 1: (*A*) is the hook end, which is used to hook the yarn and draw it through other loops of yarn (*called stitches*); (*B*) is the throat, a shaped area that helps you slide the stitch up onto (*C*) the working area; (*D*) is the fingerhold, a flattened area that helps you grip the hook comfortably, usually with your thumb and middle

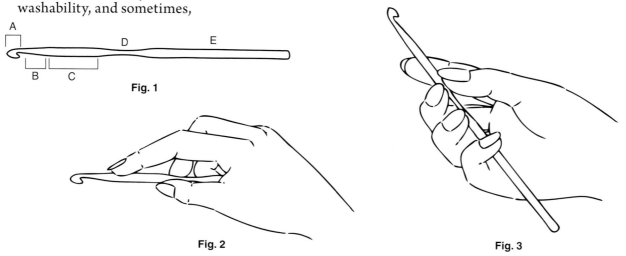

Fig. 1

Fig. 2

Fig. 3

finger; and (E) is the handle, which rests under your fourth and little fingers and provides balance for easy, smooth work.

It is important that every stitch is made on the working area, never on the throat (which would make the stitch too tight) and never on the fingerhold (which would stretch the stitch).

The hook is held in the right hand, with the thumb and third finger on the fingerhold and the index finger near the tip of the hook (Fig. 2).

The hook should be turned slightly toward you, not facing up or down. Fig. 3 shows how the hook is held, viewing from underneath the hand. The hook should be held firmly, but not tightly.

LESSON 2:
Chain Stitch
(abbreviated ch)

Crochet usually begins with a series of chain stitches called a beginning or foundation chain. Begin by making a slip knot on the hook about 6 inches from the free end of the yarn. Loop the yarn as shown in Fig. 4.

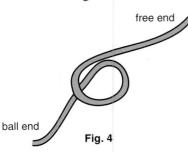

free end

ball end

Fig. 4

Insert the hook through center of loop and hook the free end (Fig. 5).

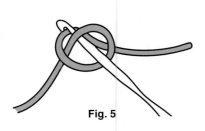

Fig. 5

Pull this through and up onto the working area of the hook (Fig. 6).

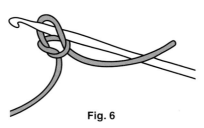

Fig. 6

Pull the free yarn end to tighten the loop (Fig. 7).

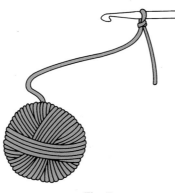

Fig. 7

The loop on the hook should be firm, but loose enough to slide back and forth easily on the hook. Be sure you still have about a 6-inch yarn end. Hold the hook, now with its slip knot, in your right hand (Fig. 8).

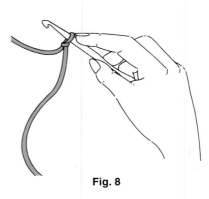

Fig. 8

Now let's make the first chain stitch.

Step 1: Hold the base of the slip knot with the thumb and index finger of your left hand, and thread yarn from the skein over the middle finger (Fig. 9) and under the remaining fingers of the left hand (Fig. 9a).

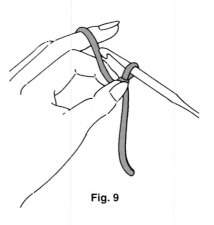

Fig. 9

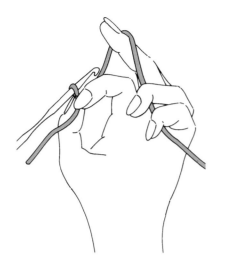

Fig. 9a

Your middle finger will stick up a bit to help the yarn feed smoothly from the skein/ball, and the other fingers help maintain an even tension on the yarn as you work.

Hint: As you practice, you can adjust the way your left hand holds the yarn to however is most comfortable for you.

Step 2: Bring the yarn over the hook from back to front and hook it *(Fig. 10)*.

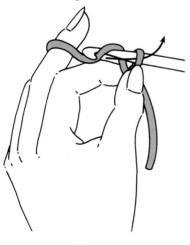

Fig. 10

Draw hooked yarn through the loop of the slip knot on the hook and up onto the working

area of the hook *(see arrow on Fig. 10)*; you have now made one chain stitch *(Fig. 11)*.

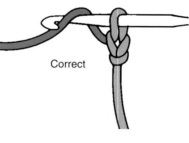

one chain stitch

Fig. 11

Step 3: Again bring the yarn over the hook from back to front *(Fig. 12a)*.

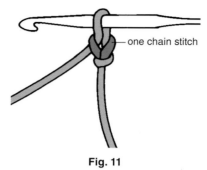

Correct

Fig. 12a

Note: Take care not to bring yarn from front to back (Fig. 12b).

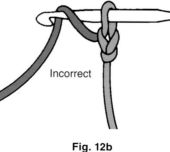

Incorrect

Fig. 12b

Hook it and draw through loop on the hook: You have made another chain stitch *(Fig. 13)*.

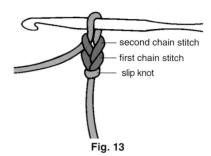

second chain stitch
first chain stitch
slip knot

Fig. 13

Repeat step 3 for each additional chain stitch, being careful to move the left thumb and index finger up the chain close to the hook after each new stitch or two *(Fig. 14a)*. This helps you control the work.

Note: Fig 14b shows the incorrect way to hold the stitches.

Also, be sure to pull each new stitch up onto the working area of the hook.

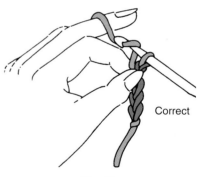

Correct

Fig. 14a

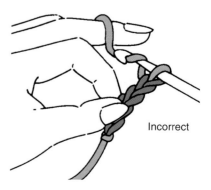

Incorrect

Fig. 14b

The working yarn and the work in progress are always held in your left hand.

Practice making chains until you are comfortable with your grip of the hook and the flow of the yarn. In the beginning your work will be uneven, with some chain stitches loose and others tight. While you're learning, try to keep the chain stitches loose. As your skill increases, the chain should be firm, but not tight, with all chain stitches even in size.

Hint: As you practice, if the hook slips out of a stitch, don't get upset! Just insert the hook again from the front into the center of the last stitch taking care not to twist the loop (Fig. 15).

When you are comfortable with the chain stitch, draw your hook out of the last stitch and pull out the work back to the beginning. Now you've learned the important first step of crochet: the beginning chain.

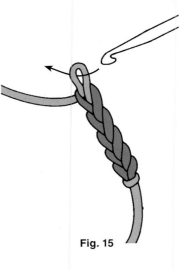

Fig. 15

LESSON 3:
Working Into the Chain

Once you have worked the beginning chain, you are ready to begin the stitches required to make any project. These stitches are worked into the foundation chain. For practice, make six chains loosely.

Hint: When counting your chain stitches at the start of a pattern—which you must do very carefully before continuing—note that the loop on the hook is never counted as a stitch, and the starting slip knot is never counted as a stitch (Fig. 16).

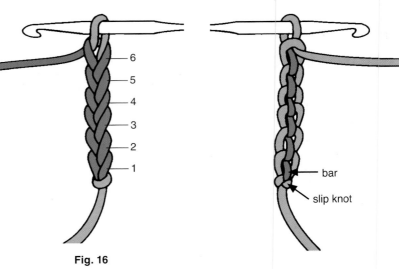

Fig. 16

Fig. 17

Now stop and look at the chain. The front looks like a series of interlocking "V's" (Fig. 16), and each stitch has a bump or ridge at the back (Fig. 17).

You will never work into the first chain from the hook. Depending on the stitch, you will work into the second, third, fourth, etc. chain from the hook. The instructions will always state how many chains to skip before starting the first stitch.

When working a stitch, insert hook from the front of the chain, through the center of the "V" and under the corresponding bump on the back of the same stitch (*Fig. 18*).

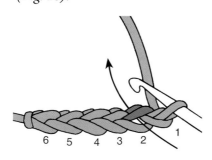

Fig. 18

Excluding the first stitch, you will work into every stitch in the chain unless the pattern states differently, but not into the starting slip knot (*Fig. 18a*). Be sure that you do not skip that last chain at the end.

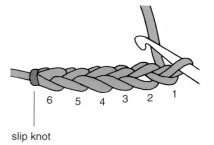

Fig. 18a

LESSON 4:
Single Crochet (abbreviated sc)

Most crochet is made with variations on just four different stitches: single crochet, double crochet, half double crochet and treble crochet. The stitches differ mainly in height, which is varied by the number of times the yarn is wrapped around the hook. The shortest and most basic of these stitches is the single crochet stitch.

WORKING ROW 1

To practice, begin with the chain of six stitches made in Lesson 3 and work the first row of single crochet as follows:

Step 1: Skip first chain stitch from hook. Insert hook in the second chain stitch through the center of the "V" and under the back bump; with middle finger of left hand, bring yarn over the hook from

back to front, and hook the yarn (*Fig. 19*).

Fig. 19

Draw yarn through the chain stitch and well up onto the working area of the hook. You now have two loops on the hook (*Fig. 20*).

Fig. 20

Step 2: Again bring yarn over the hook from back to front, hook it and draw it through both loops on the hook (*Fig. 21*).

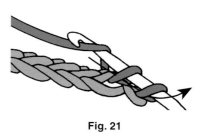

Fig. 21

One loop will remain on hook, and you have made one single crochet (*Fig. 22*).

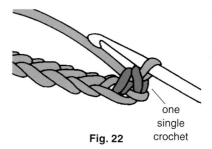

Fig. 22   one single crochet

Step 3: Insert hook in next chain stitch as before, hook the yarn and draw it through the chain stitch; hook the yarn again and draw it through both loops. You have made another single crochet.

Rep Step 3 in each remaining chain stitch, taking care to work in the last chain stitch, but not in the slip knot. You have completed one row of single crochet, and should have five stitches in the row. Fig. 23 shows how to count the stitches.

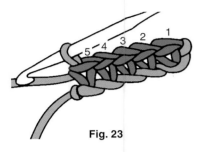

Fig. 23

Hint: As you work, be careful not to twist the chain; keep all the "V"s facing you.

WORKING ROW 2

To work the second row of single crochet, you need to turn the work in the direction of the arrow (*counterclockwise*), as shown in Fig. 24, so you can work back across the first row.

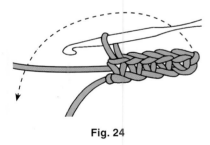

Fig. 24

Do not remove the hook from the loop as you do this (*Fig. 24a*).

Now you need to bring the yarn up to the correct height to work the first stitch. So, to raise the yarn, chain one (*this is called a turning chain*).

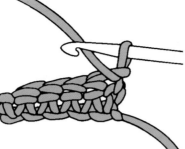

Fig. 24a

This row, and all the following rows of single crochet, will be worked into a previous row of single crochet, not into the beginning chain as you did before. Remember that when you worked into the starting chain, you inserted the hook through the center of the "V" and under the bump. This is only done when working into a starting chain.

To work into a previous row of crochet, insert the hook under both loops of the previous stitch, as shown in Fig. 25, instead of through the center of the "V".

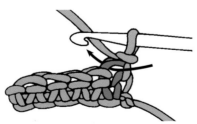

Fig. 25

The first single crochet of the row is worked in the last stitch of the previous row (*Fig. 25*), not into the turning chain. Work a single crochet into each single crochet to the end, taking care to work in each stitch, especially the last stitch, which is easy to miss (*Fig. 26*).

Fig. 26

Stop now and count your stitches; you should still have five single crochet on the row (*Fig. 27*).

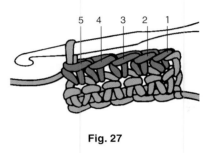

Fig. 27

Hint: When you want to pause to count stitches, check your work, have a snack or chat on the phone, you can remove your hook from the work—but do this at the end of a row, not in the middle. To remove the hook, pull straight up on the hook to make a long loop (Fig. 28). Then withdraw the hook and put it on a table or other safe place (sofas and chairs have a habit of eating crochet hooks). Put work in a safe place so loop is not pulled out. To begin work again, just insert the hook in the big loop (don't twist the loop), and pull on the yarn from the skein to tighten the loop.

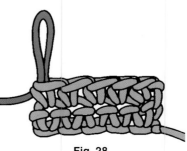

Fig. 28

To end row 2, after the last single crochet, turn the work counterclockwise.

Here is the way instructions for row two might be written in a pattern:

Note: *To save space, a number of abbreviations are used. For a list of abbreviations used in patterns, see page 127.*

Row 2: Ch 1, sc in each sc across, turn.

WORKING ROW 3

Row 3 is worked exactly as you worked row 2. Here are the instructions as they would be given in a pattern:

Row 3: Rep row 2.

Now wasn't that easy? For practice, work three more rows, which means you will repeat row 2 three times more.

Hint: *Try to keep your stitches as smooth and even as possible. Remember to work loosely rather than tightly and to make each*

stitch well up on the working area of the hook. Be sure to turn at the end of each row and to check carefully to be sure you've worked into the last stitch of each row.

Count the stitches at the end of each row; do you still have five? Good work.

Hint: *What if you don't have five stitches at the end of a row? Perhaps you worked two stitches in one stitch, or skipped a stitch. Find your mistake, then just pull out your stitches back to the mistake; pulling out in crochet is simple. Just take out the hook and gently pull on the yarn. The stitches will come out easily; when you reach the place where you want to start again, insert the hook in the last loop (taking care not to twist it) and begin.*

FASTENING OFF

It's time to move on to another stitch, so let's fasten off your single crochet practice piece, which you can keep for future reference. After the last stitch of the last row, leaving a 6-inch end, cut the yarn. As you did when you took your

hook out for a break, draw the hook straight up, but this time draw the yarn cut end completely through the stitch. Photo A shows an actual sample of six rows of single crochet to which you can compare your practice rows. It also shows how to count the stitches and rows.

Photo A

Now you can put the piece away, and it won't pull out *(you might want to tag this piece as a sample of single crochet).*

LESSON 5:
Double Crochet (abbreviated dc)

Double crochet is a taller stitch than single crochet. To practice, first chain 14 stitches loosely. Then work the first row of double crochet as follows:

WORKING ROW 1

Step 1: Bring yarn once over the hook from back to front (*as though you were going to make another chain stitch*); skip the first three chains from the hook, then insert hook in the fourth chain (*Fig. 29*).

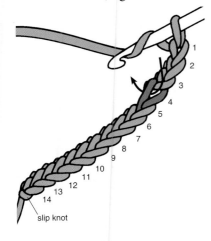

Fig. 29

Remember not to count the loop on the hook as a chain. Be sure to go through the center of the "V" of the chain and under the bump at the back, and do not twist the chain.

Step 2: Hook yarn and draw it through the chain stitch and up onto the working area of the hook: you now have three

loops on hook (*Fig. 30*).

Fig. 30

Step 3: Hook yarn and draw through first 2 loops on the hook (*Fig. 31*).

Fig. 31

You now have 2 loops on the hook (*Fig. 32*).

Fig. 32

Step 4: Hook yarn and draw through both loops on the hook (*Fig. 33*).

You have now completed one double crochet and one loop remains on the hook (*Fig. 34*).

Repeat Steps 1 through 4 in each chain stitch across (*except in Step 1, work in next chain, don't skip three chains*).

Fig. 33

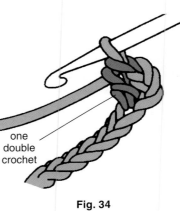

one double crochet

Fig. 34

When you've worked a double crochet in the last chain, pull out your hook and look at your work. Then count your double crochet stitches: There should be 12 of them, counting the first three chain stitches you skipped at the beginning of the row as a double crochet (*Fig. 35*).

Fig. 35

Hint: In working double crochet on a beginning chain row, the three chains skipped before making the first double crochet are usually counted as a double crochet stitch.

Turn the work counterclockwise before beginning row 2.

WORKING ROW 2

To work row 2, you need to bring the thread up to the correct height for the next row. To raise the yarn, chain three *(this is called the turning chain)*.

The three chains in the turning chain just made count as the first double crochet of the new row, so skip the first double crochet and work a double crochet in the second stitch. Be sure to insert hook under top two loops of stitch: Figs. 36a and 36b indicate

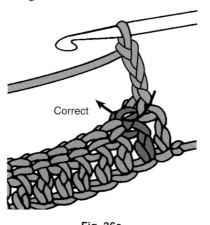

Fig. 36a

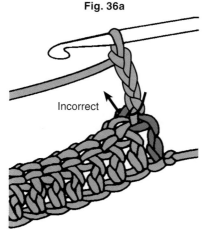

Fig. 36b

the correct and incorrect placement of this stitch.

Work a double crochet in each remaining stitch across the previous row; at the end of each row, be sure to work the last double crochet in the top of the turning chain from the previous row. Be sure to insert hook in the center of the "V" *(and back bump)* of the top chain of the turning chain *(Fig. 37)*. Stop and count your double crochets; there should be 12 stitches. Now, turn.

Fig. 37

Here is the way the instructions might be written in a pattern:

Row 2: Ch 3, dc in each dc across, turn. *(12 dc)*

WORKING ROW 3

Row 3 is worked exactly as you worked row 2.

In a pattern, instructions would read:

Row 3: Rep row 2.

For practice, work three more rows, repeating row 2. At the end of the last row, fasten off the yarn as you did for the single crochet practice piece. Photo B shows a sample of six rows of double crochet and how to count the stitches and rows.

Photo B

BREAK TIME!

Now you have learned the two most-often-used stitches in crochet. Since you've worked so hard, it's time to take a break. Walk around, relax your hands, have a snack or just take a few minutes to release the stress that sometimes develops when learning something new.

LESSON 6:
Half Double Crochet (abbreviated hdc)

Just as its name implies, this stitch eliminates one step of double crochet and works up about half as tall.

To practice, chain 13 stitches loosely.

WORKING ROW 1

Step 1: Bring yarn once over hook from back to front, skip the first two chains, then insert hook in the third chain from the hook (*Fig. 38*).

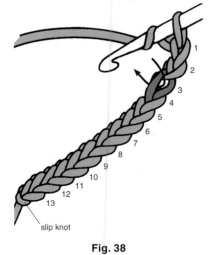

Fig. 38

Remember not to count the loop on the hook as a chain.

Step 2: Hook yarn and draw it through the chain stitch and up onto the working area of the hook. You now have three loops on the hook.

Fig. 39

Step 3: Hook yarn and draw it through all three loops on the hook in one motion (*Fig. 40*).

Fig. 40

You have completed one half double crochet and one loop remains on the hook (*Fig. 41*).

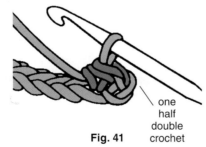

Fig. 41

one half double crochet

In next chain stitch, work a half double crochet as follows:

Step 1: Bring yarn over hook from back to front, insert hook in next chain.

Step 2: Hook yarn and draw it through the chain stitch and up onto the working area of the hook. You now have three loops on the hook.

Step 3: Hook yarn and draw it through all three loops on the hook in one motion.

Repeat the previous three steps in each remaining chain stitch across. Stop and count your stitches: You should have 12 half double crochets, counting the first two chains you skipped at the beginning of the row as a half double crochet (*Fig. 42*).

Fig. 42

Turn your work.

WORKING ROW 2

Like double crochet, the turning chain counts as a stitch in half double crochet (*unless your pattern specifies otherwise*). Chain two, skip the first half double crochet of the previous row and work a half double in the second stitch (*Fig. 43*) and in each remaining stitch across the previous row. At the end of the row, chain two and turn.

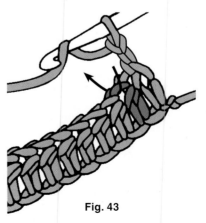

Fig. 43

Here is the way the instructions might be written in a pattern:

Row 2: Ch 2, hdc in each hdc across, turn. *(12 hdc)*

WORKING ROW 3

Row 3 is worked exactly as you worked row 2.

For practice, work three more rows, repeating row 2. Be sure to count your stitches carefully at the end of each row. When the practice rows are completed, fasten off. Photo C shows a sample of six rows of half double crochet and how to count the stitches and the rows.

Photo C

LESSON 7:
Treble Crochet (abbreviated tr)

Treble crochet is a tall stitch that works up quickly and is fun to do. To practice, first chain 15 stitches loosely. Then work the first row as follows:

WORKING ROW 1

Step 1: Bring yarn twice over the hook *(from back to front)*, skip the first four chains, then insert hook into the fifth chain from the hook *(Fig. 44)*.

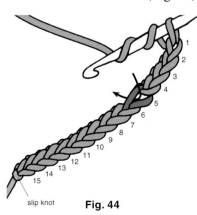

Fig. 44

Step 2: Hook yarn and draw it through the chain stitch and up into the working area of the hook; you now have four loops on the hook *(Fig 45)*.

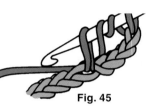

Fig. 45

Step 3: Hook yarn and draw it through the first two loops on the hook *(Fig. 46)*.

Fig. 46

You now have three loops on the hook *(Fig 46a)*.

Fig. 46a

Step 4: Hook yarn again and draw it through the next two loops on the hook *(Fig. 47)*.

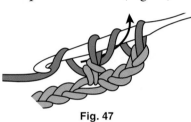

Fig. 47

Two loops remain on the hook *(Fig. 47a)*.

Fig. 47a

Step 5: Hook yarn and draw it through both remaining loops on the hook *(Fig. 48)*.

Fig. 48

You have now completed one treble crochet and one loop remains on the hook *(Fig. 49)*.

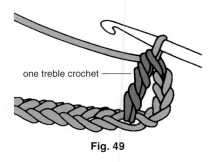

one treble crochet

Fig. 49

In next chain stitch work a treble crochet as follows:

Step 1: Bring yarn twice over the hook (*from back to front*); insert hook in the next chain (*Fig. 50*).

Fig. 50

Step 2: Hook yarn and draw it through the chain stitch and up onto the working area of the hook; you now have four loops on the hook.

Step 3: Hook yarn and draw it through the first two loops on the hook.

You now have three loops on the hook.

Step 4: Hook yarn again and draw it through the next two loops on the hook.

Two loops remain on the hook.

Step 5: Hook yarn and draw it through both remaining loops on the hook.

Repeat the previous five steps in each remaining chain stitch across. When you've worked a treble crochet in the last chain, count your stitches: There should be 12 of them, counting the first four chains you skipped at the beginning of the row as a treble crochet (*Fig. 51*); turn work.

Fig. 51

Hint: In working the first row of treble crochet, the four chains skipped before making the first treble crochet are always counted as a treble crochet stitch.

WORKING ROW 2
Chain four to bring your yarn up to the correct height, and to count as the first stitch of the row. Skip the first stitch and work a treble crochet in the second stitch (*Fig. 52*).

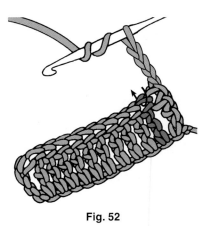

Fig. 52

Work a treble crochet in each remaining stitch across

previous row; be sure to work last treble crochet in the top of the turning chain from the previous row. Count stitches: Be sure you still have 12 stitches; turn work.

Hint: Remember to work last treble crochet of each row in turning chain of previous row. Missing this stitch in the turning chain is a common error.

Here is the way the instructions might be written in a pattern:

Row 2: Ch 4, tr in each tr across, turn. (*12 tr*)

WORKING ROW 3
Work row 3 exactly as you worked row 2.

For practice, work three more rows, repeating row 2. At the end of the last row, fasten off the yarn. Photo D shows a sample of six rows of treble crochet and how to count the stitches and rows.

Photo D

LESSON 8:
Slip Stitch (abbreviated sl st)

This is the shortest of all crochet stitches and is really more a technique than a stitch. Slip stitches are usually used to move yarn across a group of stitches without adding height, or they may be used to join work.

MOVING YARN ACROSS STITCHES
Chain 10.

WORKING ROW 1
Double crochet in the fourth chain from hook (see page 111) and in each chain across. Turn work. On the next row, you are going to slip stitch across the first four stitches before beginning to work double crochet again.

WORKING ROW 2
Instead of making three chains for the turning chain as you would usually do for a second row of double crochet, this time just chain one. The turning chain-one does not count as a stitch; therefore, insert hook under both loops of first stitch, hook yarn and draw it through both loops of stitch and loop on the hook (Fig. 53); one slip stitch made.

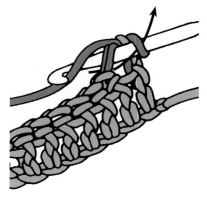

Fig. 53

Work a slip stitch in the same manner in each of the next three stitches. Now we're going to finish the row in double crochet; chain three to get yarn at the right height (the chain-three counts as a double crochet), then work a double crochet in each of the remaining stitches. Look at your work and see how we moved the yarn across with slip stitches, adding very little height (Fig. 54).

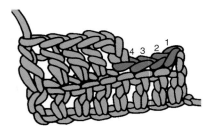

Fig. 54

Fasten off and save the sample.

Here is the way the instructions might be written in a pattern.

Row 2: Sl st in each of next 4 dc, ch 3, dc in each rem dc, fasten off. (5 dc)

Hint: When slip stitching across stitches, always work very loosely.

JOINING STITCHES
JOINING A CHAIN INTO A CIRCLE
Chain six, then insert hook through the first chain you made (next to the slip knot—Fig. 55).

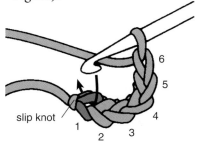

Fig. 55

Hook yarn and draw it through the chain and through the loop on hook; you have now joined the six chains into a circle or a ring. This is the way many motifs, such as granny squares, are started. Cut yarn and keep this practice piece as a sample.

JOINING THE END OF A ROUND TO THE BEGINNING OF THE SAME ROUND
Chain six; join with a slip stitch in first chain you made to form a ring. Chain three; work 11 double crochet in the ring; insert hook in third chain of beginning chain three (Fig. 56); hook yarn and

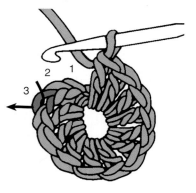

Fig. 56

draw it through the chain and through the loop on the hook; you have now joined the round. Cut yarn and keep this piece as a sample.

Here is the way the instructions might be written in a pattern:

Rnd 1: Ch 3, 11 dc in ring, join in 3rd ch of beg ch-3.

LESSON 9:
Stitch Sampler

Now you've learned the basic stitches of crochet! Wasn't it fun? The hard part is over!

To help you understand the difference in the way single crochet, half double crochet, double crochet and treble crochet stitches are worked, and the difference in their heights, let's make one more sample.

Chain 17 loosely. Taking care not to work too tightly, single crochet in the second chain from hook and in each of the next three chains; work a half double crochet in each of the next four chains; work a double crochet in each of the next four chains; work a treble crochet in each of the next four chains. Fasten off. Your work should look like Photo E.

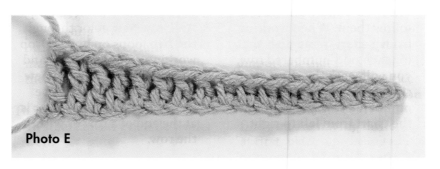

Photo E

LESSON 10:
Bead Crochet

Now that you have mastered the basic crochet stitches, it is time to learn a technique which will give your work some sparkle.

Bead crochet is a simple technique in which you add beads to your work as you crochet the stitches.

In a pattern, you will be given the size beads necessary for the project.

Before beginning the project, slide the beads on the yarn. Follow the pattern until you are instructed to add a bead. To add a bead, simply slide a bead up to the loop on the hook *(Fig. 57)*.

Now work the next stitch. Depending on which side of the work you want the bead to be, you will work the next

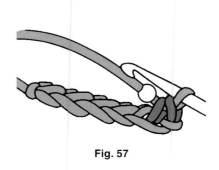

Fig. 57

stitch either behind the bead, to have the bead on the side of your work facing you, or in front of the bead, to have the bead on the side away from you.

LESSON 13:
Special Helps

INCREASING & DECREASING

Shaping is done by increasing, adding stitches to make the crocheted piece wider, or decreasing, subtracting stitches to make the piece narrower.

Note: Make a practice sample by chaining 15 stitches loosely and working four rows of single crochet with 14 stitches in each row. Do not fasten off at end of last row. Use this sample swatch to practice the following method of increasing stitches.

Increasing: To increase one stitch in single, half double, double or treble crochet, simply work two stitches in one stitch. For example, if you are working in single crochet and you need to increase one stitch, you would work one single crochet in the next stitch; then you would work another single crochet in the same stitch.

For practice: On sample swatch, turn work and chain one. Single crochet in each of first two stitches; increase in next stitch by working two single crochets in stitch *(Fig. 59)*.

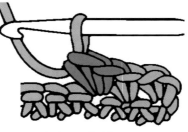

single crochet increase

Fig. 59

Repeat increase in each stitch across row to last two stitches; single crochet in each of next two stitches. Count your stitches: You should have 24 stitches. If you don't have 24 stitches, examine your swatch to see if you have increased in each specified stitch.

Rework the row if necessary.

Increases in half double, double and treble crochet are shown in Figs. 59a, 59b and 59c.

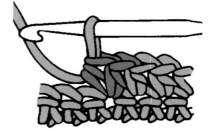

half double crochet increase

Fig. 59a

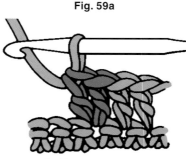

double crochet increase

Fig. 59b

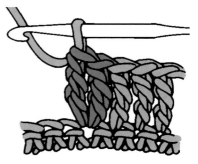

treble crochet increase

Fig. 59c

Note: Make another practice sample by chaining 15 loosely and working four rows of single crochet. Do not fasten off at end of last row. Use this sample swatch to practice the following methods of decreasing stitches.

Decreasing: This is how to work a decrease in the four main stitches. Each decrease gives one fewer stitch than you had before.

Single crochet decrease (sc dec): Insert hook and draw up a loop in each of the next two stitches (three loops now on hook), hook yarn and draw through all three loops on the hook *(Fig. 60)*.

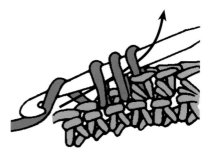

Fig. 60

Single crochet decrease made (*Fig. 61*).

Fig. 61

Double crochet decrease (dc dec): Work a double crochet in the specified stitch until two loops remain on the hook (*Fig. 62*).

Fig. 62

Keeping these two loops on hook, work another double crochet in the next stitch until three loops remain on hook; hook yarn and draw through all three loops on the hook (*Fig. 63*).

Fig. 63

Double crochet decrease made (*Fig. 64*).

Fig. 64

Half double crochet decrease (hdc dec): Yo, insert hook in specified stitch and draw up a loop, three loops remain on the hook (*Fig. 65*).

Fig. 65

Keeping these three loops on hook, yo and draw up a loop in the next stitch (*five loops now on hook*), hook yarn and draw through all five loops on the hook (*Fig. 66*).

Fig. 66

Half double crochet decrease made (*Fig. 67*).

Fig. 67

Treble crochet decrease (tr dec): Work a treble crochet in the specified stitch until two loops remain on the hook (*Fig. 68*).

Fig. 68

Keeping these two loops on hook, work another triple crochet in the next stitch until 3 loops remain on the hook; hook yarn and draw through all loops on the hook (*Fig. 69*).

Fig. 69

Treble crochet decrease made (*Fig. 70*).

Fig. 70

JOINING NEW THREAD
Never tie or leave knots! In crochet, yarn ends can be easily worked in and hidden because of the density of the stitches. Always leave at least 6-inch ends when fastening off yarn just used and when joining new yarn. If a flaw or a knot appears in the yarn while you are working from a skein, cut out the imperfection and rejoin the yarn.

Whenever possible, join new yarn at the end of a row. To do this, work the last stitch with the old yarn until two loops remain on the hook, then complete the stitch with the new yarn (*Fig. 71*).

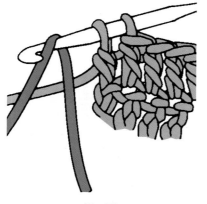

Fig. 71

To join new yarn in the middle of a row, when about 12 inches of the old yarn remains, work several more stitches with the old yarn, working the stitches over the end of new yarn (*Fig. 72 shown in double crochet*). Then change yarns in stitch as previously explained.

Fig. 72

Continuing with the new yarn, work the following stitches over the old yarn end.

FINISHING
A carefully crocheted project can be disappointing if the finishing has been done incorrectly. Correct finishing techniques are not difficult, but do require time, attention and knowledge of basic techniques.

Weaving in ends: The first procedure of finishing is to securely weave in all yarn ends. Thread a size 16 steel tapestry needle with yarn, then weave running stitches either horizontally or vertically on the wrong side of work. First weave about 1 inch in one direction and then ½ inch in the reverse direction. Be sure yarn doesn't show on right side of work. Cut off excess yarn. Never weave in more than

one yarn end at a time.

Sewing seams: Edges in crochet are usually butted together for seaming instead of layered, to avoid bulk. Do not sew too tightly—seams should be elastic and have the same stretch as the crocheted pieces.

Carefully matching stitches and rows as much as possible, sew the seams with the same yarn you used when crocheting.

Invisible seam: This seam provides a smooth, neat appearance because the edges are woven together invisibly from the right side. Join vertical edges, such as side or sleeve seams, through the matching edge stitches, bringing the yarn up through the posts of the stitches (*Fig. 73*).

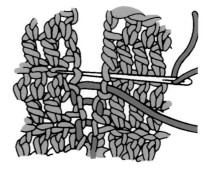

Fig. 73

If a firmer seam is desired, weave the edges together through both the tops and the posts of the matching edge stitches.

Backstitch seam: This method gives a strong, firm edge and is used when the seam will have a lot of stress or pull on it. Hold the pieces with right sides together and then sew through both thicknesses as shown *(Fig. 74)*.

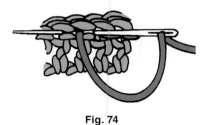

Fig. 74

Overcast seam: Strips and pieces of afghans are frequently joined in this manner. Hold the pieces with right sides together and overcast edges, carefully matching stitches on the two pieces *(Fig. 75)*.

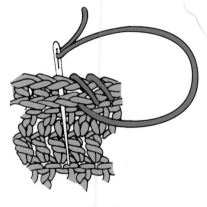

Fig. 75

Edges can also be joined in this manner, using only the back loops or the front loops of each stitch *(see page 173)*.

Crocheted seam: Holding pieces with right sides together, join yarn with a slip stitch at right-side edge. Loosely slip stitch pieces together, being sure

not to pull stitches too tightly *(Fig. 76)*. You may wish to use a hook one size larger than the one used in the project.

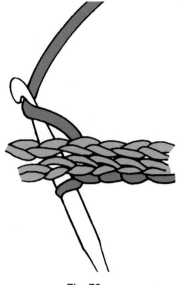

Fig. 76

EDGING

Single crochet edging: A row of single crochet worked around a completed project gives a finished look. The instructions will say to "work a row of single crochet, taking care to keep work flat." This means you need to adjust your stitches as you work. To work the edging, insert hook from front to back through the edge stitch and work a single crochet. Continue evenly along the edge. You may need to skip a row or a stitch here or there to keep the edging from rippling, or add a stitch to keep the work from pulling.

When working around a corner,

it is usually necessary to work at least three stitches in the corner center stitch to keep the corner flat and square *(Fig. 77)*.

Fig. 77

Reverse single crochet edging: A single crochet edging is sometimes worked from left to right for a more dominant edge. To work reverse single crochet, insert hook in stitch to the right *(Fig. 78)*, hook yarn and draw through stitch, hook yarn and draw through both loops on the hook *(Fig. 79)*.

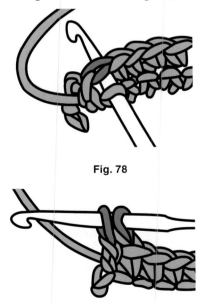

Fig. 78

Fig. 79

LESSON 14: Reading Patterns

ABBREVIATIONS

Crochet patterns are written in a special language full of abbreviations, asterisks, parentheses, brackets and other symbols and terms. These short forms are used so instructions will not take up too much space. They may seem confusing at first, but once understood, they are really easy to follow.

SYMBOLS

An asterisk is used to mark the beginning of a portion of instructions which will be worked more than once; thus, "rep from * twice" means after working the instructions once, repeat the instructions following the asterisk twice more (3 *times in all*).

[ ] Brackets are used to enclose instructions which should be repeated the number of times specified immediately following the brackets: "[2 sc in next dc, sc in next dc] twice." Brackets are also used to indicate additional or clarifying information for multiple sizes: "child's size 2 [4, 6]"; "Row 29 [31, 33]."

( ) Parentheses are used to set off and clarify a group of stitches that are to be worked all into the same space or stitch, such as: "(2 dc, ch 1, 2 dc) in corner sp."

ABBREVIATIONS

beg	begin/beginning	g	gram(s)
bpdc	back post double crochet	hdc	half double crochet
bpsc	back post single crochet	inc	increase/increases/increasing
bptr	back post treble crochet	lp(s)	loop(s)
CC	contrasting color	MC	main color
ch	chain stitch	mm	millimeter(s)
ch-	refers to chain or space previously made (i.e., ch-1 space)	oz	ounce(s)
		pc	popcorn
		rem	remain/remaining
		rep	repeat(s)
ch sp	chain space	rnd(s)	round(s)
cl	cluster	RS	right side
cm	centimeter(s)	sc	single crochet
dc	double crochet	sk	skip(ped)
dec	decrease/decreases/decreasing	sl st	slip stitch
		sp(s)	space(s)
		st(s)	stitch(es)
dtr	double treble crochet	tog	together
fpdc	front post double crochet	tr	treble crochet
		trtr	triple treble crochet
fpsc	front post single crochet	WS	wrong side
		yd(s)	yard(s)
fptr	front post treble crochet	yo	yarn over

{ } Braces are used to indicate a set of repeat instructions within a bracketed or parenthetical set of repeat instructions: "[{ch 5, sc in next shell sp} twice, ch 5, sk next dc]"; "({dc, ch 1} 5 times, dc) in next ch sp."

TERMS

Front loop (front lp) is the loop toward you at the top of the stitch (*Fig. 80*).

Back loop (back lp) is the loop away from you at the top of the stitch (*Fig. 80*).

Post is the vertical part of the stitch (*Fig. 80*).

Work even means to continue to work in the pattern as established, without increasing or decreasing.

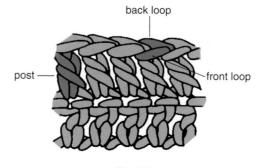

back loop

post

front loop

Fig. 80

Wrong side (WS): The side of the work that will not show when project is in use.

Right side (RS): The side that will show.

Right-hand side: The side nearest your right hand as you are working.

Left-hand side: The side nearest your left hand as you are working.

Right front: The piece of a garment that will be worn on the right-hand side of the body.

Left front: The piece of a garment that will be worn on the left-hand side of the body.

LESSON 15:
Gauge

We've left this until last, but it really is the single most important thing in crochet.

If you don't work to gauge, your crocheted projects may not be the correct size, and you may not have enough yarn to finish the project.

Gauge means the number of stitches per inch and rows per inch that result from a specified yarn worked with a specified-size hook. Since everyone crochets differently—some loosely, some tightly, some in-between—the measurements of individual work can vary greatly when using the same-size hook and yarn. It is **your responsibility** to make sure you achieve the gauge specified in the pattern.

Hook sizes given in instructions are merely guides and should never be used without making a 4-inch-square sample

swatch to check gauge. Make the sample gauge swatch using the size hook, yarn and stitch specified in the pattern. If you have more stitches per inch than specified, try again using a larger-size hook. If you have fewer stitches per inch than specified, try again using a smaller-size hook. Do not hesitate to change to a larger-or smaller-size hook, if necessary, to achieve gauge. If you have the correct number of stitches per inch, but cannot achieve the row gauge,

adjust the height of your stitches. This means that after inserting the hook to begin a new stitch, draw up a little more yarn if your stitches are not tall enough—this makes the first loop slightly higher; draw up less yarn if your stitches are too tall. Practice will help you achieve the correct height.

This photo shows how to measure your gauge.

Metric Conversion Charts

METRIC CONVERSIONS				
yards	x	.9144	=	metres (m)
yards	x	91.44	=	centimetres (cm)
inches	x	2.54	=	centimetres (cm)
inches	x	25.40	=	millimetres (mm)
inches	x	.0254	=	metres (m)

centimetres	x	.3937	=	inches
metres	x	1.0936	=	yards

INCHES INTO MILLIMETRES & CENTIMETRES (Rounded off slightly)

inches	mm	cm	inches	cm	inches	cm	inches	cm
1/8	3	0.3	5	12.5	21	53.5	38	96.5
1/4	6	0.6	5 1/2	14	22	56	39	99
3/8	10	1	6	15	23	58.5	40	101.5
1/2	13	1.3	7	18	24	61	41	104
5/8	15	1.5	8	20.5	25	63.5	42	106.5
3/4	20	2	9	23	26	66	43	109
7/8	22	2.2	10	25.5	27	68.5	44	112
1	25	2.5	11	28	28	71	45	114.5
1 1/4	32	3.2	12	30.5	29	73.5	46	117
1 1/2	38	3.8	13	33	30	76	47	119.5
1 3/4	45	4.5	14	35.5	31	79	48	122
2	50	5	15	38	32	81.5	49	124.5
2 1/2	65	6.5	16	40.5	33	84	50	127
3	75	7.5	17	43	34	86.5		
3 1/2	90	9	18	46	35	89		
4	100	10	19	48.5	36	91.5		
4 1/2	115	11.5	20	51	37	94		

CROCHET HOOKS CONVERSION CHART

Canada/U.S.	1/B	2/C	3/D	4/E	5/F	6/G	8/H	9/I	10/J	10½/K	N
Metric (mm)	2.25	2.75	3.25	3.5	3.75	4.25	5	5.5	6	6.5	9.0

STITCH GUIDE

STITCH ABBREVIATIONS

beg . . . . begin/begins/beginning
bpdc . . . . back post double crochet
bpsc . . . . back post single crochet
bptr . . . . back post treble crochet
CC . . . . contrasting color
ch(s) . . . . chain(s)
ch- . . . . refers to chain or space
previously made (i.e., ch-1 space)
ch sp(s) . . . . chain space(s)
cl(s) . . . . cluster(s)
cm . . . . centimeter(s)
dc . . . . double crochet (singular/plural)
dc dec . . . . double crochet 2 or more
stitches together, as indicated
dec . . . . decrease/decreases/decreasing
dtr . . . . double treble crochet
ext . . . . .extended
fpdc . . . . front post double crochet
fpsc . . . . front post single crochet
fptr . . . . front post treble crochet
g . . . . gram(s)
hdc . . . . half double crochet
hdc dec . . . . .half double crochet 2 or more
stitches together, as indicated
inc . . . . increase/increases/increasing
lp(s) . . . . .loop(s)
MC . . . . .main color
mm . . . . millimeter(s)
oz . . . . ounce(s)
pc . . . . popcorn(s)
rem . . . . remain/remains/remaining
rep(s) . . . . .repeat(s)
rnd(s) . . . . round(s)
RS . . . . right side
sc . . . . single crochet (singular/plural)
sc dec . . . . .single crochet 2 or more
stitches together, as indicated
sk . . . . .skip/skipped/skipping
sl st(s) . . . . slip stitch(es)
sp(s) . . . . space(s)/spaced
st(s) . . . . stitch(es)
tog . . . . .together
tr . . . . treble crochet
trtr . . . . .triple treble
WS . . . . wrong side
yd(s) . . . . .yard(s)
yo . . . . yarn over

YARN CONVERSION

OUNCES TO GRAMS	GRAMS TO OUNCES
1 . . . . 28.4	25 . . . . ⅞
2 . . . . 56.7	40 . . . . 1⅔
3 . . . . 85.0	50 . . . . 1¾
4 . . . . 113.4	100 . . . . 3½

UNITED STATES		UNITED KINGDOM
sl st (slip stitch)	=	sc (single crochet)
sc (single crochet)	=	dc (double crochet)
hdc (half double crochet)	=	htr (half treble crochet)
dc (double crochet)	=	tr (treble crochet)
tr (treble crochet)	=	dtr (double treble crochet)
dtr (double treble crochet)	=	ttr (triple treble crochet)
skip	=	miss

Reverse single crochet (reverse sc): Ch 1, sk first st, working from left to right, insert hook in next st from front to back, draw up lp on hook, yo, and draw through both lps on hook.

Chain (ch): Yo, pull through lp on hook.

Single crochet (sc): Insert hook in st, yo, pull through st, yo, pull through both lps on hook.

Double crochet (dc): Yo, insert hook in st, yo, pull through st, [yo, pull through 2 lps] twice.

Front loop (front lp) Back loop (back lp)

Front Loop   Back Loop

Front post stitch (fp): Back post stitch (bp): When working post st, insert hook from right to left around post of st on previous row.

Back   Front

Post of Stitch

Half double crochet (hdc): Yo, insert hook in st, yo, pull through st, yo, pull through all 3 lps on hook.

Double treble crochet (dtr): Yo 3 times, insert hook in st, yo, pull through st, [yo, pull through 2 lps] 4 times.

Slip stitch (sl st): Insert hook in st, pull through both lps on hook.

Chain color change (ch color change) Yo with new color, draw through last lp on hook.

Double crochet color change (dc color change) Drop first color, yo with new color, draw through last 2 lps of st.

Treble crochet (tr): Yo twice, insert hook in st, yo, pull through st, [yo, pull through 2 lps] 3 times.

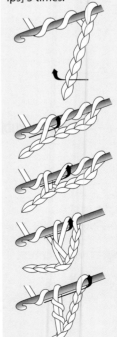

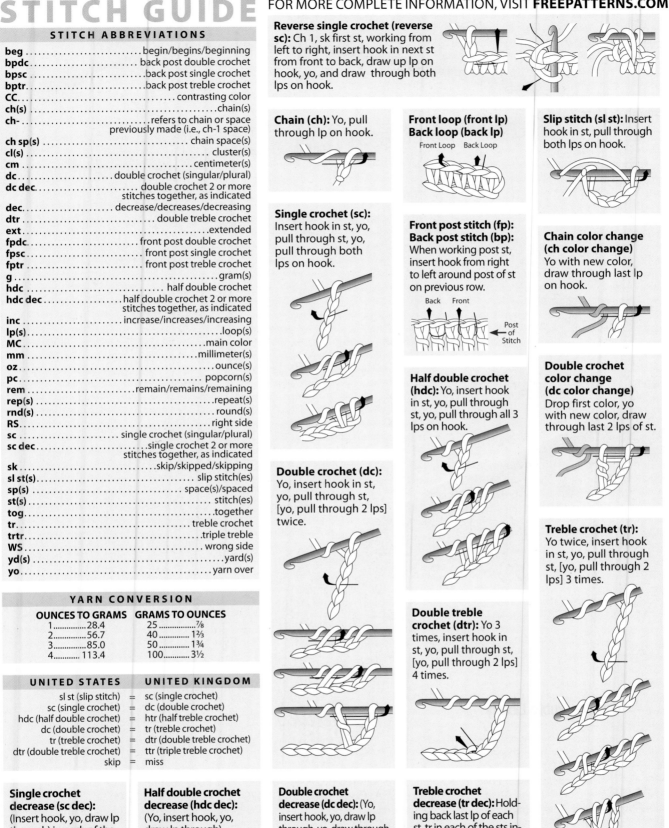

Single crochet decrease (sc dec): (Insert hook, yo, draw lp through) in each of the sts indicated, yo, draw through all lps on hook.

Example of 2-sc dec

Half double crochet decrease (hdc dec): (Yo, insert hook, yo, draw lp through) in each of the sts indicated, yo, draw through all lps on hook.

Example of 2-hdc dec

Double crochet decrease (dc dec): (Yo, insert hook, yo, draw lp through, yo, draw through 2 lps on hook) in each of the sts indicated, yo, draw through all lps on hook.

Example of 2-dc dec

Treble crochet decrease (tr dec): Holding back last lp of each st, tr in each of the sts indicated, yo, pull through all lps on hook.

Example of 2-tr dec

4-11-12

Annie's Attic®

101 Crochet Stitch Patterns & Edgings is published by DRG, 306 East Parr Road, Berne, IN 46711.
Printed in USA. Copyright © 2012 DRG.

RETAIL STORES: If you would like to carry this pattern book or any other DRG publications, visit DRGwholesale.com

Every effort has been made to ensure that the instructions in this publication are complete and accurate.
We cannot, however, take responsibility for human error, typographical mistakes or variations in individual work.
Please visit AnniesCustomerCare.com to check for pattern updates.

ISBN: 978-1-59635-406-7
Library of Congress: 2011962229

1 2 3 4 5 6 7 8 9